Social Mobility Myths

Social Mobility Myths

Peter Saunders

Civitas: Institute for the Study of Civil Society
London

First Published June 2010

© Civitas 2010
55 Tufton Street
London SW1P 3QL
Civitas is a registered charity (no. 1085494)
and a company limited by guarantee, registered in
England and Wales (no. 04023541)

email: books@civitas.org.uk

ISBN 978-1-906837-14-3

Independence: Civitas: Institute for the Study of Civil Society is a registered educational charity (No. 1085494) and a company limited by guarantee (No. 04023541). Civitas is financed from a variety of private sources to avoid over-reliance on any single or small group of donors.

All publications are independently refereed. All the Institute's publications seek to further its objective of promoting the advancement of learning. The views expressed are those of the authors, not of the Institute.

Typeset by
Civitas

Printed in Great Britain by
Cromwell Press Group
Trowbridge, Wiltshire

"Aim high
For though you may not reach the sky
You will most certainly reach the mountaintops"

Teacher's inscription in my father's autograph book on the day he left school at the age of 14 in the summer of 1939.

After leaving school, my father started work as a factory operative. At 17 he joined the RAF, and after the war he enlisted at a teacher training college. He went on to complete a successful and rewarding career as a sports and science teacher, which included almost 10 years teaching in Zambia, Uganda and Namibia.

This book is dedicated to my father, and to all those teachers, past and present, who encourage children to rise above their circumstances, to take advantage of the opportunities that are available to them, and to exploit their talent to the full.

Contents

Author

Peter Saunders was until 1999 Professor of Sociology at the University of Sussex, where he is still Professor Emeritus. He has also held visiting academic posts at universities in Australia, Germany, New Zealand and the United States. In 1999 he moved to Australia to become Research Manager at the Australian Institute of Family Studies in Melbourne, and in 2001 he moved to Sydney to take up the position as Social Research Director at the Centre for Independent Studies. In 2008 he returned to the UK where he now works as an independent writer and consultant. His books include *A Nation of Home Owners; Capitalism — A Social Audit; Social Theory and the Urban Question; Introduction to British Politics; Privatisation and Popular Capitalism* and *Australia's welfare habit and how to kick it.* He recently published two reports for the London-based think tank, Policy Exchange: an analysis of the family tax and benefits system in Britain, and a critique of the government's child poverty targets.

More details of his work can be found at www.petersaunders.org.uk.

Acknowledgements

I owe a special debt of gratitude to Dr Rod Bond at the University of Sussex with whom I worked closely in the 1990s analysing social mobility data, and who was mainly responsible for developing the path model outlined in Figure 1 (p. 86). Some of my early work was supported by a small personal research grant from the Economic and Social Research Council; the Centre for Independent Studies in Sydney supported me when I needed to respond to criticisms a few years later; and Civitas in London has funded this latest return to the topic. I am particularly grateful to David Green, the Director of Civitas, who first suggested I have another crack at these issues, and to Claire Daley at Civitas, who has done an excellent job editing the manuscript. I am also grateful for comments, help, suggestions or guidance at various times in the past from Bob Blackburn, Alan Buckingham, Ian Deary, Geoff Evans, David Hitchin, Gordon Marshall, Trevor Noble, Geoff Payne, Ken Prandy, and Peter Shepherd, although none of these people bears any responsibility for what follows.

Introduction

Almost 30 years ago, Professor Peter Bauer, an economist at the London School of Economics, attacked what he termed the 'British obsession' with class. Britain, he said, sees itself as a peculiarly class-divided nation when in reality we are a remarkably open society. According to Bauer, there is a strong and pervasive myth in Britain that class divisions are sharper and more enduring than in other western industrialised countries, and that social movement between classes is rare and difficult to achieve. Seeking to refute such claims, he appealed to anecdotal and sociological evidence to try to show that Britain has in reality been a relatively open society for a long time.[1]

Back in 1981, when Bauer published this essay, there was not a lot of evidence on contemporary rates of 'social mobility' for him to draw upon. But in the years since then, sociologists and economists have been busy documenting and analysing people's social and economic origins and destinations. As a result, we now know a great deal about movement up the ladders and down the snakes of our society. We have accurate measures of how many people born to lowly parents end up in high status positions, and how many children with privileged beginnings fail to make the grade. We know how likely it is that somebody born to poor parents will end up affluent, or that someone born to rich parents will end up penniless.

What is 'social mobility'?

Social mobility refers to the movement of individuals from one position in society to another. This movement may be measured in the course of their own lives (e.g. by comparing their first job after leaving school with the job they end up doing later in their career), in which case it represents 'intra-generational mobility'; or it may be assessed by comparing their current position with the position occupied by their parents when they were the same age ('inter-generational mobility').

The 'positions' that are compared may be based on occupational rankings, incomes, education, or some measure of social class or socio-economic status. Social mobility is said to occur when individuals move from a lower to a higher position ('upward mobility'), or from a higher to a lower one ('downward mobility') on one of these scales.

We can also make reasonably reliable claims about why people succeed or fail. Much of what happens to individuals in the course of their lifetimes is down to chance and idiosyncratic circumstances, but social science can make some generalisations. We can assess whether hard work makes much of a difference to where people end up; how far intelligence drives personal success; whether formal education and paper qualifications matter most; or whether the advantages bequeathed by one's parents—being born with a 'silver spoon' in your mouth—are what really count in the end.

In 1996, I wrote a short book which assessed the evidence on social mobility in Britain that was then available to us. Entitled *Unequal But Fair?*,[2] the book basically supported Bauer's claim that Britain is a relatively open society in which people's achievements mainly reflect their own efforts and talents. I suggested that, while competition for high income and high status employment did not take place on a completely level playing field, modern Britain was a much more open and 'meritocratic' society than most commentators seemed willing to acknowledge. In particular, the positions which individuals achieved for themselves in modern Britain had a lot more to do with their abilities and their hard work than with the social advantages or disadvantages bestowed upon them by accident of birth.

What is a 'meritocracy'?

The word was coined in 1958 by Michael Young in his widely-read and influential book, *The Rise of the Meritocracy 1870-2033*. Young detected in post-war Britain a growing emphasis on social recruitment based, not on social origins, but on individual talent and motivation, and he anticipated a time when the higher occupational positions in British society would all be filled by the most able and hard-working individuals. He was himself somewhat worried about such an outcome, for he thought a meritocratic society would run into severe problems as a result of the disaffection of the less talented and less committed majority congregating at the base of the social pyramid.[3]

Young defined 'merit' as consisting of 'intelligence and effort together'.[4] In a meritocracy, in other words, intellectual ability and hard work alone determine social placement.

2

In *Unequal But Fair?*, I showed that rates of social mobility were not markedly different from what we would expect to find in a perfectly meritocratic society, where people's achieved socio-economic status depended entirely on their ability and hard work. I also demonstrated that, to the extent that Britain fell short of the meritocratic ideal, circumstances of birth operated mainly to prevent less able, higher class children from failing, rather than to stop more able, lower class people from succeeding. I concluded that, if you are reasonably bright and motivated, there is little in modern Britain stopping you from succeeding in life (even if some rich kids do get an unfair start).

When I wrote that book, interest in social mobility was mainly limited to a small circle of academics, nearly all of whom were sociologists. When the book came out, most of them either ignored it, or attempted to discredit my arguments. Their response was not unexpected, for academic sociology in Britain was (and still is) heavily dominated by a left-leaning ideology. Only three per cent of British sociology professors vote Conservative, and nine out of ten of them describe their political views as 'hard left' or 'moderate left'.[5] This uniformity has produced an ideological orthodoxy about social mobility that stifles the whole discipline in Britain.

Left-wing academics like to believe that Britain is a class-ridden, unfair society in which children born into modest circumstances have the odds massively stacked against them. I call this belief the '*SAD thesis*', for it assumes that 'social advantage and disadvantage' conferred at birth is what shapes people's destinies. The SAD thesis is directly opposed to the meritocracy thesis, which suggests that even children born into the humblest of circumstances can succeed if they are bright and they work hard. The left-wing sociological establishment regards any suggestion that occupational selection in Britain might be taking place on broadly meritocratic principles as literally incredible. The SAD thesis is their 'dominant paradigm' through which all evidence gets filtered, and against which all arguments are evaluated.[6]

In the decade and a half since *Unequal But Fair?* was published, interest in social mobility has mushroomed. Economists as well as sociologists have begun to study it, and politicians as well as academics have started to take a serious interest in it. Unfortunately, however, the SAD thesis has continued to dominate most research and discussion, be it academic or political.

Academic research on social mobility developed into a major growth industry after the election of the Blair government in 1997, and this is when economists joined sociologists in crunching the numbers. However, the two disciplines tend to measure mobility in different ways, and this has led to some confusion. Sociologists like to examine movement in and out of different 'social class' positions, for they see 'class' as a powerful indicator of people's material life chances.[7] Economists, on the other hand, focus much more narrowly on people's incomes, so they measure the number of people who end up in a different income band than that of their parents. As we shall see in Chapter 3, this difference of focus between the two styles of research has generated some interesting, and puzzling, discrepancies in findings.

The election of the Blair government also marked the beginning of serious political interest in social mobility, for 'New Labour' identified the encouragement of social mobility as one of its core objectives. Very soon, ministers were lining up to emphasise their commitment to the meritocratic ideal:[8]

- 'The government's fight is on behalf of hard-earned merit, not easy prizes' (David Miliband, Schools Ministers, 2004);

- '...a Britain where merit is the key to success, where the only thing that counts is not where you come from but what you are' (Tony Blair, Prime Minister, 2001);

- 'We must create a society where ability flows to the top irrespective of an individual's background' (Ruth Kelly, Secretary of State for Education, 2005).

Over the last 15 years, concern about social mobility has increasingly come to dominate public policy debates. All three main political parties have published reports on it, the Blair and Brown governments have set up various inquiries to investigate it, and in November 2008, the Cabinet Office Strategy Unit announced that: 'Improving social mobility is at the heart of the government's agenda.'[9]

Many trees have been sacrificed...

A number of government reports have been produced on social mobility—or the lack of it. The Cabinet Office published *Getting On, Getting Ahead* in November 2008. This reported that social mobility has not been improving, and it set out a series of proposals, most of which were later incorporated into a White Paper, aimed at 'capturing' more quality jobs and increasing individual opportunities. This was swiftly followed in May 2009 by Alan Milburn's report on 'fair access to the professions', *Unleashing Aspiration.*[10] In his foreword to this report, Milburn (former Cabinet Minister) claimed that 'birth, not worth, has become more and more a determinant of people's life chances' and he described Britain as 'a closed-shop society.' The report was widely welcomed in Parliament. Then, in January 2010, Harriet Harman's National Equality Panel published its 450 page report, *An Anatomy of Economic Inequality in the UK,* which claimed that intergenerational mobility in the UK is 'low' and that large inequalities make it more difficult for people to improve their situations.[11]

Not surprisingly, perhaps, this new political enthusiasm for promoting social mobility has been heavily influenced by the beliefs, assumptions and prejudices that underpin most of the academic work done in this area. In particular, the prevailing SAD thesis has been imported from academe into the public policy realm, and this has generated four, core 'social mobility myths' which are now routinely repeated but rarely, if ever, challenged in public discussions of this issue:

- The myth that Britain is 'a closed shop society' in which life chances are heavily shaped by the class you are born into;[12]

- The myth that social mobility, already limited, is now getting worse;

- The myth that differences of ability between individuals either do not exist, or are irrelevant in explaining differential rates of success;

- The myth that governments can increase social mobility via top-down social re-engineering within the education system and forcing more income redistribution.

Most politicians accept these myths. They assume that social mobility in Britain is very limited, when it is not, and that class origins count much more than personal effort and talent in shaping people's destinies, when they do not. If anything, these SAD myths have strengthened over the last ten to 15 years, not least because the most influential group of economists to have joined in this debate has claimed, not only that mobility is limited, but that it has started to *decline*.

This claim has attracted widespread attention and has been taken seriously by politicians in all parties. On the Labour Party side, old-style class warriors have seized on apparent evidence of falling mobility rates to justify their belief in root-and-branch, top-to-bottom social reform to sweep away traditional class privileges. And the Conservatives have grasped at apparent evidence of falling mobility rates as a weapon with which to attack Labour's record in office.[13] Both sides have been predisposed to believe what the academics are telling them. The result is that politicians from all parties now commonly express their sense of outrage that a class-ridden, closed society is becoming even more class-ridden and even more closed.

This is all deeply depressing. Almost 15 years after publishing what I hoped would be an important corrective to the prevailing, and deeply misleading, sociological orthodoxy about social mobility, this orthodoxy has not only survived, but has strengthened its claims and extended its grip beyond academe and into the very heart of government. With all three parties now apparently convinced that bright children born into humble backgrounds are being blocked by an unfair class system from realising their potential, and that things are getting worse rather than better, the scene has been set for yet another bout of expensive (and ultimately fruitless) social engineering aimed at dismantling the imagined inequities of the British class system.

There is no shortage of big ideas around Westminster and Whitehall about how to do this. We are being told that universities must be forced to admit children from poorer backgrounds on lower grades while discriminating against those educated in private schools. Higher education must be expanded still further, and loans for students from poorer backgrounds must be subsidised, or replaced by grants. Parents must be prevented from exercising choice over which state school their children attend, with enrolments determined by local lotteries. There must be an end to streaming by ability, more children must be made to stay at school past the age of 16, and more taxpayer money must be spent on vocational training. Early years interventions must be extended and strengthened, and even more money must be redistributed to low income families in the never-ending mission to 'abolish child poverty'. Government must also somehow ensure that the number of 'good jobs' (i.e. middle class, non-manual jobs requiring degrees and other paper qualifications) continues to grow, so that working class children can continue to be siphoned out of their lowly backgrounds to fill them.

All this and more is currently being proposed in order to address the 'social mobility problem'. Yet careful scrutiny of the evidence demonstrates that this 'problem' either does not exist, or has been hugely exaggerated. Before we commit to spending millions of pounds we cannot afford on policies to remove unfair blockages to talented and hard-working people from less privileged backgrounds, we should at least make sure the blockages really are there in the first place.

In the chapters that follow, I have dusted down those parts of *Unequal But Fair?* that have stood the test of time, and have supplemented them with new and updated materials gathered from a comprehensive, secondary analysis of the contemporary research literature. My original intention was simply to produce an updated, second edition of the book, but so much new material has been published since 1996 that I have ended up with an almost entirely new work which addresses the new political circumstances in which the social mobility debate is now being played out.[14]

My aim in publishing this new book is ridiculously ambitious, for I hope to convince our political masters that much of what they believe (or say they believe) about social mobility in this country is either false or more complicated than they think. I hope I have a bit more success with the politicians today than I had with the sociological establishment 15 years ago. All I ask of the reader is that you approach the material that follows with an open and critical mind.

1

Absolute Mobility: How Tall are the Ladders; How Long are the Snakes?

In this book I seek to demonstrate, against the received wisdom, that occupational selection and recruitment in Britain is much more meritocratic than most of us realise or care to believe. However, I enter three important caveats at the outset.

First, I am not looking at recruitment into the very top ('elite') positions in British society. There is no open competition for the position as the next monarch, nor do you stand much chance of accumulating the sort of assets enjoyed by the Duke of Westminster. Even entry to a Labour cabinet seems a lot easier if you are the brother, son, grandson, daughter, niece or spouse of a Labour Party Grandee.[1] I do not, therefore, claim that *all* positions in British society are filled through open competition on the basis of individual ability and effort. My focus is on the 99 per cent of jobs below the elite stratum, rather than on the one per cent which constitute it.[2]

Secondly, most research on social mobility compares the job (or earnings) that somebody achieves in adulthood with the job (or earnings) that their parent or parents had at roughly the same age. Such analysis obviously depends on two generations of families having paid work that can be compared. This means that research on social mobility has very little to say about what happens to children growing up in jobless, long-term welfare-dependent households. Even though their numbers have become increasingly significant over the last 40 years, those without jobs (and/or whose parents were without jobs) tend to be dropped from social mobility studies altogether, or they get subsumed into bigger categories and their distinctiveness is lost.

This literature cannot, in consequence, tell us much about recruitment into, and out of, what has been called 'the underclass', even though this is probably where our major problem lies. The social mobility literature does not generally trace the life trajectories of people who were abused or neglected as children, whose parents were drug abusers, criminals or alcoholics, or whose fathers played no part in their upbringing. These may well be crucial, early disadvantages, but they are overlooked by the simple 'social class' categories and earnings bands on which mobility researchers tend to focus. I shall have something to say at the end of the book about improving the opportunities for these children, but most of the research evidence we shall be looking at is focused on the 'mainstream' of British society (the 'working class' and the 'middle class'), rather than on its margins (the 'underclass').

Thirdly, even focusing only on the mainstream, I shall not claim that Britain is a *perfect* meritocracy. The various advantages and disadvantages associated with different social class origins do still play some part in influencing people's occupational chances—sociologists have not been completely wrong or deluded. The point, however, is that Britain is much more meritocratic than is generally believed. Class origins are not very important, nor are the supposed advantages (such as private schooling) enjoyed by children born to more affluent or better-placed parents particularly significant in shaping outcomes. To the extent that it is possible to predict somebody's occupational destiny, it is their ability and their motivation that matters much more than the social class into which they were born. In modern Britain, if you are bright and committed, you are likely to succeed in the occupational system irrespective of what your parents did for a living, and although things are not perfect and the playing field is not completely level, this means that our society is relatively open. We are much closer to achieving a meritocracy than most pundits or politicians seem to suppose.

The origins of the SAD thesis

The British sociological community has long argued that competition for more favoured social and economic positions is skewed in favour of those born into higher classes, and that the dice are heavily loaded against anyone born into the working class. Because sociologists are paid to write about this sort of thing, and nobody else (until recently) had the evidence or the analytical tools necessary to study it, their views have largely shaped what we all think we know about the British class system.

Down the years, sociologists have argued that the meritocracy ideal is no more than an elaborate illusion, an ideological confidence trick designed to win legitimacy for a socially unjust system that perpetuates middle class privilege. No less an esteemed figure than Professor Tawney once dismissed the idea of equal competition in Britain as 'obviously a jest',[3] and the generation of eminent British sociologists that followed him was happy to reinforce his sentiments:

> The social class system... operates, largely, through the inheritance of property, to ensure that each individual maintains a certain social position, determined by his birth and irrespective of his particular abilities... Most social mobility takes place between social levels which are close together... The vast majority of people still remain in their class of origin... In Britain, all manner of ancient institutions and modes of behaviour—the aristocracy, the public schools, Oxbridge, differences of speech and accent, the relationships of the 'old boy' network—frustrate mobility.
>
> (Professor Tom Bottomore, 1965)[4]

> Those who fear a 'meritocratic' society in which everyone, starting more or less equally, would be judged on 'merit' alone, need not therefore be unduly alarmed: the race is still rigged—against the working class competitors... the upper and middle class... is still largely self-recruiting and therefore to a marked degree socially cohesive.
>
> (Professor Ralph Miliband, 1969)[5]

> The chances that those born into different social classes will stay in those classes are still very high. Though there is a good deal of mobility, most of it is, in fact, very short range mobility. The myths of 'long distance' mobility—from 'log cabin to President'—are, overwhelmingly, myths as far as the life chances of the mass of the population are concerned... it is far too simplistic to describe modern society as predominantly 'achievement-oriented'.
>
> (Professor Peter Worsley, 1970)[6]

> Virtually all movement, whether upward or downward, inter- or intra-generational, across the non-manual/manual division is 'short-range'... There has not been much change in rates of mobility between manual and non-manual labour over the period since World War I.
>
> (Professor Anthony Giddens, 1973)[7]

> People are a good deal more likely to stay at roughly the same level as their fathers than they would be if there were 'perfect mobility'... Those born into the top strata have enormous advantages in respect of their job prospects—as in respect of so much else—over all others; not least in this country. Long distance movement especially—from bottom to top, as well as from top to bottom—is uncommon. Most individual mobility is far more modest; and much of it stays on one side or the other of the conventional dividing line between white- and blue-collar work... Movement up and down the ladder is inhibited by sharp inequalities of opportunity'.
>
> (Professor John Westergaard with Henrietta Resler, 1975)[8]

This uniformity of opinion made a huge impression on the discipline of sociology as it became established in Britain in the first 30 years after the Second World War, and its legacy remains with us to this day. People like Bottomore, Giddens and Worsley were core figures in the development of sociology in this country. They were the people who set the agenda, did the research and wrote the text books. When they said something, it was passed on to subsequent generations of students as received truth. And *all* these eminent professors assured us that the race in Britain was rigged, meritocracy was a myth, and what determined where you ended up in life was not your ability or your determination but the colour of your father's club tie.

These claims did not rest solely on ideology. There was one piece of research to which all these professors appealed, a study of ten thousand men conducted by Professor David Glass and his colleagues at the London School of Economics in the late 1940s.[9] This study found that social mobility across anything more than a very short range of occupational statuses was uncommon, and that most people stayed in the class into which they had been born. These results were constantly recycled in the sociological literature of the 1950s, 60s and 70s and, they underpinned the unanimity with which the profession supported and promoted the SAD thesis.

There were, however, two major problems with Glass's study. The first was that, by the 1970s, his data were badly out-of-date. It is in the nature of all social mobility research that we are always looking back over our shoulders, at how things were a generation ago, rather than how they are now. To compare the achievements of a current cohort with those of their parents, you have to wait for them to grow up and establish themselves in careers, by which time 30 or 40 years have passed. But the Glass data were even more dated than that. The study had been carried out back in the 1940s on a sample of men, most of whom had left school and started work long before the Second World War broke out. More than two-thirds of the fathers of these men had first entered the labour market when Queen Victoria was still on the throne.

Glass himself warned that the patterns of mobility he documented between these two generations were unlikely to tell us much about post-war British society, for social reforms (like the 1944 Education Act) which were explicitly designed to open up social opportunities had had

11

little chance to take effect by the time he conducted his research. But later generations of sociologists largely ignored these warnings and treated Glass's findings as if they were still applicable to the society they were living in. Glass's data were uncritically recycled for the next 30 years, and generations of sociology students were taught that Britain was a relatively closed society in which the upper and middle classes could secure their position for the next generation, and where talented children born into the working class had little realistic prospect of significant upward movement, even into relatively low-status white collar jobs.[10]

The second, and even more serious, problem with Glass's study was that its statistics were badly flawed. Geoff Payne[11] calculated that, taking account of (a) the expansion in white-collar and contraction in blue-collar jobs during the twentieth century, and (b) the higher fertility rates in working class than in middle class families during this period, the data reported by Glass could only have been valid if the number of white collar jobs had declined by 18 per cent in the course of a generation. In reality, however, the number of white collar jobs *increased* over this period by 17 per cent. Glass's findings, in other words, were *impossible* given the occupational changes documented by censuses through the first 50 years of this century.

Payne stops short of accusing Glass of manufacturing his data, but he does note with some frustration the reluctance of later sociologists to treat Glass's findings with the critical scepticism they so clearly deserved. His explanation for this applies today just as much as it did 30 or 40 years ago: 'Almost without exception, sociological writers on social class in Britain have adopted a political stance on the Left. When Glass wrote that there was little upward social mobility, it reinforced everything else that they knew about the class system. There was no incentive, therefore, to challenge his results.'[12] For 30 years, from the 1950s to the 70s, sociologists in Britain accepted statistics which could not possibly be true because they fitted with their own ideological prejudices. Those prejudices remain just as strong today.

The orthodoxy is finally challenged

Eventually, Glass's conclusions were challenged. In what remains the single most important and rigorous survey of social mobility in Britain, carried out in 1972, Professor John Goldthorpe and colleagues at

Nuffield College, Oxford, finally demonstrated, much to their own surprise, that the fundamental assumptions of so much post-war British sociology were quite wrong. Based upon a national representative sample of ten thousand men, and defining social classes according to the income and degree of authority and autonomy typically associated with the occupations they held, Goldthorpe found that a lot of people were moving between social classes. This was true comparing the occupations of sons with those of their fathers ('intergenerational mobility'), and comparing people's first occupations with those achieved later in their careers ('intragenerational mobility').

Goldthorpe's social classes

Goldthorpe identified seven (and with sub-divisions, eleven) different social classes, but most of these can be collapsed into three main classes:

The *service class* (sometimes also referred to as the 'salariat'), which consists mainly of professional, managerial and high-level administrative positions, as well as the owners of large companies. This service class is divided into 'higher' and 'lower' grades (classes I and II);

The *intermediate classes*, consisting of routine white-collar grades (class IIIa), personal service workers (IIIb), owners of small-scale enterprises (the 'petty bourgoisie', or class IV), who are in turn divided into those with (IVa) and without (IVb and IVc) employees; and lower-grade technicians and supervisors (class V);

The *working class*, which is made up of skilled (class VI), and semi-skilled and unskilled (class VIIa) manual employees exercising no supervisory functions, as well as agricultural workers (VIIb).

The various intermediate classes are not ranked against each other, so movement between them does not count as upward or downward social mobility.

Analysing movement between his three principal classes, Goldthorpe found that almost half of his sample (49 per cent) ended up in a social class which was different from that into which they had been born.

Flying in the face of sociological orthodoxy, which insisted that higher class parents were adept at passing on their privileged position to their children, Goldthorpe showed that there was substantial movement down as well as up this class system. He also challenged the long-standing belief that any movement that does occur takes place over a very short range, for he found that long-range movement was common, including movement both ways across the supposed white-collar/blue-collar 'barrier'. While 59 per cent of the sons of service class fathers had retained their class position, 26 per cent of them had fallen into the intermediate classes, and 15 per cent had dropped all the way down to the working class. Similarly, while 57 per cent of working class sons had remained in the class to which they had been born, 27 per cent had entered intermediate class positions and 16 per cent had risen into the service class.

Thinking that these results may have been a peculiar product of the long post-war boom, and that the onset of recession from the mid-1970s might have led to a subsequent diminution in social mobility rates, Goldthorpe went on in 1983 to conduct a follow-up study using data collected from the general election survey of that year. Again, his results came as a surprise, for rather than narrowing, the chances of social movement had expanded in the intervening decade! By 1983, more than half (53 per cent) of the sample had changed classes, and the chances of working class upward movement had markedly improved (the proportion of working class sons entering the service class had risen from 16 per cent to 22 per cent, while the proportion remaining where they had started had fallen from 57 percent to 47 per cent).

This evidence on what Goldthorpe termed 'absolute rates' of social mobility was enough to convince him that the post-war sociological orthodoxy was wrong. What he called the 'closure thesis' (which held that top positions are self-recruiting), the 'buffer zone thesis' (which claimed that movement across long distances was severely restricted), and the 'counterbalance thesis' (which suggested that any increase in inter-generational social mobility chances had been countered by a decrease in the opportunities for intra-generational movement), were all flatly refuted by his findings.

Later studies by other researchers have confirmed Goldthorpe's findings. At the University of Essex, Gordon Marshall and his colleagues found in a national survey in the 1980s that one-third of all men and women in the service class had started life in the manual working class.[13] In Scotland, Geoff Payne found that membership of

14

even the most senior levels of the service class was extremely unstable, only a minority managing to retain such positions across more than one generation, and 14 per cent of service class children ending up in manual working class jobs.[14] And drawing on a series of general election surveys which have gathered occupational data, Heath and Payne found that, throughout the twentieth century, half or more of the population changed its class position relative to that of their fathers. Fewer than half of all men born to class I fathers stayed in class I themselves, and four in ten of the sons born to unskilled manual worker fathers achieved movement into white collar or service class positions. Upward mobility was extensive throughout the century, and became increasingly common as the middle class expanded (Table 1).

Table 1
Absolute inter-generational social mobility rates for different birth cohort in the UK during the twentieth century (percentages)[15]

Birth cohort	Pre-1900	1900-1909	1910-1919	1920-1929	1930-1939	1940-1949	1950-1959
Men							
Upwardly mobile	27	29	30	39	38	42	42
Downwardly mobile	20	21	20	17	18	19	13
Women							
Upwardly mobile	24	22	27	23	29	32	36
Downwardly mobile	30	32	30	28	27	26	27

In recent years, we have also had access to the results of a number of national panel surveys which have followed a representative sample of the population over an extended period of time. One of these, the National Child Development Study (NCDS), has followed 17,416 individuals from their birth in one week in 1958 through to adulthood. These people were aged 46 when they were last questioned in 2004.[16] A later cohort of 16,571 people born in 1970 (the British Cohort Study, or BCS) has also been tracked, and they too have now reached an age where their achieved positions can be compared with those of their parents at an equivalent age (they were aged 34 when last contacted in 2004).[17] In both cases, a wealth of information has been gathered about class backgrounds, education, job histories and personal attributes. In addition, the British Household Panel Survey (BHPS), which began in 1991 and questions the same sample of people every year, has also been mined for the information it can reveal about social mobility.

All of these longitudinal surveys confirm that social mobility in Britain is extensive and common. Goldthorpe and Jackson[18] have analysed the 1958 and 1970 birth cohort studies and report that by age 33, 45 per cent of the men and 39 per cent of the women in the 1958 birth cohort had moved upwards relative to the social class of their parents, and 27 per cent of the men and 37 per cent of the women had moved down. For the 1970 cohort (assessed at age 30), the equivalent figures were 42 per cent (men) and 41 per cent (women) moving up, and 30 per cent (men) and 35 per cent (women) moving down.

Table 2
Working class upward mobility, and service class downward mobility, in the 1958 and 1970 birth cohorts (percentages of total men and women in samples)[19]

	Class of destination at age 30/33		
	Service class	Intermediate class	Working class
1958 Cohort			
Men:			
Service class origin	18.5	4.7	5.2
Working class origin	15.5	9.9	23.1
Women:			
Service class origin	14.2	7.1	6.0
Working class origin	12.9	15.2	23.3
1970 Cohort			
Men:			
Service class origin	22.4	7.2	4.7
Working class origin	12.4	11.4	14.5
Women:			
Service class origin	22.6	10.2	4.5
Working class origin	12.3	13.1	12.3

Source: John Goldthorpe and Michelle Jackson, 'Intergenerational class mobility in contemporary Britain', *British Journal of Sociology*, vol. 58, 2007, 525-46. Service class defined as classes I, II and IVa (small proprietors with employees); working class defined as classes VI and VII.

These results suggest that it is more unusual today for somebody to stay in the social class in which they were born than to move out of it, either up or down. Table 2 shows that, in both the 1958 and 1970 cohorts, more of the men and women born into the working class had climbed to a higher class position than had stayed put (for those born in 1970, almost twice as many were upwardly mobile than remained in the working class). Movement downwards, out of the service class, was also fairly common. In both cohorts, around one-third of the men, and almost half the women, born to service class parents failed to maintain their initial position.

Given that occupational mobility often takes place beyond the early thirties (the age at which these panel members' career achievements were measured), we can assume that total mobility (intra- as well as inter-generationally) will be even greater than these figures suggest.[20] Clearly, the experience of class mobility is widespread in Britain.

More room at the top

Looking back, nobody should perhaps have been surprised by the amount of movement uncovered by Goldthorpe, and confirmed by later surveys, for we have known for a long time that the occupational structure was shifting quite dramatically throughout the twentieth century. Before 1914 (when most of the fathers of David Glass's sample were entering work), about three-quarters of all the jobs in Britain were in manual work (basically, 'the working class' in Goldthorpe's schema), and only a quarter were 'white collar' (the 'intermediate' and 'service' classes). With the decline of manufacturing employment, the growth of state sector employment and the impact of technological change on routine jobs, these proportions have now almost completely reversed.[21]

The shrinkage of the working class and the expansion of the service class over the last hundred years had to entail recruitment of increasing numbers of working class children into the new professional and managerial positions that were being created. There had to be quite extensive upward social mobility in order for the occupational changes to take place. There was, as John Goldthorpe puts it, 'more room at the top', which meant people born into lower social strata had to be 'sucked up' into the expanding middle classes above them.

Having said that, however, it is also important to note that downward mobility has continued to be significant throughout this period. In Goldthorpe's 1972 survey, four in ten of the sons born to service class fathers ended up in a lower class than their father, and in the two birth cohort studies, the proportion is still around one-third. This is certainly not what would have been predicted from the shifts in the occupational structure. With the middle class expanding, and the working class contracting, we would not expect to find much evidence of middle class children sliding downwards, yet downward mobility has been quite marked.

When John Goldthorpe compared social mobility rates across different countries, he found that downward social mobility was actually higher in England and Scotland than in any of the other nations included in his analysis.[22] Although critics commonly claim that Britain is less fluid and open than other European countries (and particularly Scandinavia), these data on downward mobility suggest otherwise, for with an expanding middle class, it is arguably the rate of downward mobility which tells you most about how open a society really is.

How does the UK compare with other countries?

There is considerable disagreement and confusion in the literature comparing the amount of social mobility in Britain with that recorded in other western, developed countries. We would do well to heed the warning of the OECD that any such comparisons should be treated with 'a great deal of caution'.[23]

Most sociologists think mobility rates are similar across most western countries, and the 2001 review by the UK government's Performance and Innovation Unit concluded that any differences that do exist are 'modest'.[24] Economists, however, have started to disagree with this, and the 2010 report of the 'National Equality Panel' follows them in claiming that mobility rates in Britain are lower than in almost all other European countries. Not surprisingly, this dramatic claim has received a lot of media coverage.[25]

The truth is that mobility between *social class* positions appears little different in Britain than in other, comparable nations. The National Equality Panel's own data show that absolute rates of upward mobility (measured in terms of the proportion of men ending up in a higher class than their fathers) are about the same in Britain as in Ireland,

France and Germany, but are a bit lower than in the Netherlands, Italy and Scandinavia.[26] The report does not discuss downward mobility, but OECD analysis confirms that we are around the middle of the international rankings overall. This is borne out in analyses by Erikson and Goldthorpe (who put England 8th out of 15 nations, with greater fluidity than Germany, France and the Netherlands, but behind Sweden, the USA and Australia) and by Breen.[27]

The OECD also reports that Britain is more fluid than the average when we compare *educational levels* attained by parents and their children.[28] If we correlate years of schooling undertaken by children as compared with their parents, Britain's correlation of 0.31 is weaker than that in any other developed country except Denmark (i.e. our children's education is not strongly predicted by that of their parents), and we rank 6th out of 42 nations on this criterion of fluidity.[29]

The idea that Britain is lagging behind everyone else comes from economists' research on *income* mobility. An influential group of economists has found that, when we compare men's earnings with those of their parents, Britain and the USA perform poorly compared with Canada and most other European countries (i.e. there is a stronger association between parents' and children's earnings here than in other nations).[30] The report by the National Equality Panel repeats this finding. But when we inspect the data more closely, this result is unconvincing.

For a start, the most prominent of these economists, Jo Blanden, admits, 'There is a lot of uncertainty about the UK.' The problem reflects the fact that parental incomes may change markedly over time (in which case it will matter a great deal at what age parental earnings are estimated). To deal with this, parental incomes can be 'adjusted' in the light of other information, such as parents' occupation or education (so-called 'instrumental variables'). But this produces wildly differing estimates, and it is not clear which we should accept. Blanden, for example, reports one correlation between UK sons' and parents' incomes of 0.44, but notes that this seems 'extremely high' (even though it has itself been adjusted downwards from an initial 0.58) when compared with another of just 0.29. To come up with her own figure, Blanden ends up averaging the two contrasting results, but this appears wholly arbitrary, and we have no way of knowing whether or not it brings her close to a 'true' estimate.[31]

When this (adjusted, averaged, estimated) correlation is compared with those from other countries, it comes out higher than the other European countries examined, and is only exceeded by the USA. This might indicate that income mobility in Britain and the US is low compared with most of Europe, but the Standard Errors on these estimates are huge (the Standard Error gives us the likely range within which the real figure for each country lies).

Because these ranges are so great, they nearly all overlap with each other, which means the differences between most countries' estimates are not statistically significant. For example, the USA ranks very poorly while Sweden ranks quite well, but Blanden admits: 'It is impossible to statistically distinguish the estimates for Sweden and the US.' In other words, they might very well exchange places! She goes on: 'The appropriate ranking at the top end is difficult with large standard errors on the Australian, French, British and US estimates *making it unclear how these countries should be ranked.*'[32]

Finally, adding even more confusion, Blanden also acknowledges that another study, by Andrews and Leigh, has estimated income mobility for 15 countries (not including Britain) and come up with a very different set of results. On this calculation, the USA is around the middle of the rankings, beating Australia and coming close to Norway.

Clearly, when looking at income mobility statistics, we are dealing with data that contain a lot of error, where international comparisons are fraught, and where 'adjustments' and assumptions made by researchers can produce alarmingly different 'results'.

What are we to conclude from all of this? Britain seems about average on class mobility, quite open on education mobility, and its international ranking on income mobility is (in Blanden's own words) 'unclear'. It is stretching the data to the limit for the National Equality Panel to conclude from patterns like these that our 'rates of intergenerational mobility in terms of incomes are low in international terms, and in terms of occupation are below the international average'.[33]

2

Relative Mobility: Who Benefited Most from the Expansion of the Middle Class?

Clearly the British class system is a lot more open than the traditional sociological orthodoxy ever imagined. But the evidence reviewed in the previous chapter has done nothing to dissuade sociologists from their view that the British class system is rigid and relatively closed. The SAD thesis continues to dominate conventional thinking in this field, and the reason is that researchers generally prefer to focus on what they call 'relative mobility' rates than on the 'absolute mobility' statistics that we have been examining up until now.

The figures on 'absolute mobility' show a lot of movement going on, but they do not tell us how much of this is due to changes in the occupational system itself, and how much is due to greater 'fluidity' between occupational groups. In technical terminology, statistics on changing absolute mobility rates cannot distinguish 'structural mobility' from 'pure mobility'. To do this, we have to calculate 'relative mobility' rates, and when we do, many academics believe it shows that the middle classes still have the system sewn up, and that the working class is still being unfairly excluded from competing on an equal basis for the material rewards our society has to offer.

We have seen that high absolute rates of upward mobility have to some degree been driven by the expansion of the middle class and the shrinkage of the working class over the last hundred years. Mobility researchers refer to this as the 'structural' effect—upward mobility has increased because more room has opened up at the top of the system. But what they want to know is who has benefited most from this increased 'room at the top'? Has the opening up of top positions meant that working class children now enjoy the same sorts of opportunities to succeed in life as middle class children? Or have the middle classes also taken advantage of this expansion by securing their children's futures even more successfully than they did before?

Clearly, if we are concerned about improving people's life chances, this question of relative gain is secondary to the question of absolute gain. People are unlikely to care whether increased opportunities have been delivered by the expansion of middle class jobs, or a loosening of class barriers. What matters most to them is that their chance to succeed in life has improved, irrespective of whether everybody else's chances have improved by a similar degree. John Goldthorpe confirmed this in his 1972 survey where he showed that most respondents were concerned, not with whether their children's opportunities had improved relative to other people's children, but with whether their children had a better chance of succeeding today than they did in the past.

In this sense, the most important research findings are those outlined in the previous chapter. The big story is that occupational mobility has become common, and that many more people today have the opportunity to achieve a middle class lifestyle than was the case in the past.[1]

Nevertheless, the attention of researchers has become firmly fixed on relativities, not absolutes. They accept there is now greater opportunity for people to achieve a middle class position, but the test of fairness they lay down is that those at the bottom should have availed themselves of these expanded opportunities *to a greater extent* than those at the top. Only if this happens will relative mobility rates show any improvement.

Measures of relative class mobility: Disparity ratios and odds ratios

Sociologists seeking to measure relative mobility rates generally do so by calculating 'disparity ratios' and 'odds ratios'.

Disparity ratios express the relative likelihood of children from different social class origins arriving at the same social class destination. For example, if 20 per cent of those from working class backgrounds achieve middle class positions, and 60 per cent of those from middle class backgrounds achieve middle class positions, there is a 3:1 disparity ratio in the relative chances of occupational success enjoyed by middle class as compared with working class children.

Odds ratios are rather more complicated and are constructed in three stages. First, we calculate the chances of a child from a higher class position falling to a lower class. If, for example, 50 per cent of service class children retain their position while ten per cent fall all the way down to the working class, this gives them a 5:1 chance of ending up in the working class as against remaining in the service class (even though

---

the chance of remaining in the service class is even). Secondly, a similar calculation is made regarding the chances of a child from working class origins rising all the way up to a service class position as compared with the likelihood of remaining in the working class. If, say, 60 per cent of working-class children end up in working class jobs while 20 per cent make it to the top, this would give each working class child a 3:1 chance of getting to the top as against remaining where they started from. Thirdly, these two sets of disparity ratios are then expressed in relation to each other by multiplying the first by the second. In our hypothetical example, this would produce a final odds ratio of 15:1 (5:1 against service class downward mobility divided by 3:1 against working class upward mobility).

Middle class/working class disparity ratios

Having demolished the conventional sociological wisdom by demon-strating in his 1972 survey that 'absolute mobility' was widespread and extensive, it was John Goldthorpe who went on to rescue the SAD thesis by emphasising that 'relative mobility' rates did not seem to have changed much over the years.

Although large numbers of working class men had been upwardly mobile, Goldthorpe found that working class children in his sample had not improved their chances of occupational success relative to children born into higher social classes. Everybody had gained more-or-less equally from the expansion of the middle class during the twentieth century, for while it enabled more working class children to move up, it also helped more middle class children to avoid falling down. Because the expansion of top positions had been equally advantageous to the children of all social classes, the gap between them in terms of their relative chances of success was as wide as ever.

Goldthorpe concluded from this that there was 'little if any evidence of progress having been made' towards greater openness in the class system, and that 'no significant reduction in class inequalities was in fact achieved' during the post-war period, despite the expansion of educational opportunities for working class children since 1944.[2]

The relative chances of success or failure faced by the men in Goldthorpe's sample can be gauged by analysing a series of 'disparity ratios' comparing the probabilities of children from different class origins ending up in the same class destination. Goldthorpe reasoned that, if people's class origins played no part in shaping their life chances, all disparity ratios should be 1:1. In other words, a working class child should be just as likely as a middle class child to end up as a doctor or an accountant, and a middle class child should be just as likely as a working class child to end up as a shop assistant or factory operative.

What he actually found, however, was a disparity ratio of nearly 4:1, when comparing the chances of children born to service-class fathers and those born to working-class fathers each achieving a service class position in adulthood. The service class children, in other words, were about four times more likely than the working class children to end up in the middle class. A similar disparity ratio of about 4:1 was also evident when comparing their chances of ending up in a working class job, only this time, the boot was on the other foot, and the probability was that the working class child would remain in his class of origin.

By comparing different birth cohorts within his sample, Goldthorpe was able to demonstrate that these ratios had remained fairly constant over time. However, in his follow-up 1983 survey he found that the disparity in the chances of service class and working class children achieving a service class destination had apparently fallen during the previous decade from around 4:1 to around 3:1, although the disparity in their chances of ending up in a working class position had increased to almost 5:1.[3] The chances against working class success had therefore reduced, while those against middle class failure had lengthened.

Goldthorpe concluded from his evidence that there were persisting inequalities in chances of success for children from different social class origins. Similar findings were also recorded by the Essex University team when they investigated relative social mobility rates in their 1984 survey. Like Goldthorpe, they too found significant disparities in relative mobility chances, and they claimed on the basis of their results that, 'The post-war project of creating in Britain a more open society... has signally failed to secure its objective.'[4]

It is possible to calculate disparity ratios for other data sets collected since these studies were completed. I have done this in Table 3 which estimates the relative chances of 'middle class' and 'working class' males ending up in 'middle class' or 'working class' occupations, based on (a) the Heath and Payne election survey data (looking at the whole period 1964-97)[5]; (b) Breen and Goldthorpe's analysis of the two national birth cohort studies when members were aged 23 (NCDS) and 26 (BCS)[6]; and (c) my own analysis (in *Unequal But Fair?*) of the NCDS birth cohort at age 33.[7] The three sets of data have been analysed and classified in slightly different ways and are therefore not strictly comparable with each other (social class boundaries are treated differently in each case, and the ages of respondents vary),[8] and for the sake of simplicity, women have been excluded altogether (because the labour market is quite strongly gendered, women tend have a different occupational profile from men). Nevertheless, taken together with Goldthorpe's earlier (1972) findings, the figures in Table 3 provide a fairly clear guide to the scale of the mobility disparities experienced by men around the top and bottom of the British class structure towards the end of the twentieth century (I reserve to the next chapter an examination of what may have been happening since then).

Table 3
Disparity ratios comparing male middle class
and working class origins and destinations

(a) 1964-97 election surveys:

	Relative chance of being in:	
	Class I/II	Class V/VI/VII
Father class I/II	3.3	set at 1
Father class V/VI/VII	set at 1	3.5

(b) NCDS (age 23) and BCS (age 26):
NCDS:

	Relative chance of being in:	
	Class I/II	ClassVI/VII
Father class I/II	2.7	set at 1
Father class VI/VII	set at 1	2.1

BCS:

	Relative chance of being in:	
	Class I/II	Class VI/VII
Father class I/II	1.8	set at 1
Father class VI/VII	set at 1	2.2

(c) NCDS (age 33):

	Relative chance of being in:	
	Class I/II	Class IV/V
Father OPCS class I/II	2.6	set at 1
Father OPCS class IV/V	set at 1	3.8

Looking at Table 3, it is clear that men born to middle class fathers enjoy favourable mobility chances as compared with those born to working class fathers. However, none of these disparity ratios is as high as 4:1 (the figure recorded in Goldthorpe's 1972 survey), many are below 3:1, and some are less than 2:1. Remembering that we are here comparing movement right across the occupational class system (ignoring short-range upward and downward mobility of children reaching the intermediate classes), and that a disparity ratio of 1:1 would indicate no association at all between class origins and destinations, these results do not seem to indicate the existence of huge barriers to upward or downward movement.

Middle class/working class odds ratios

A second measure of relative mobility rates is provided by odds ratios, and they can be dramatically large. To calculate an odds ratio, we basically multiply together two different disparity ratios. This produces a single, summary statistic which is intended to measure 'overall fluidity' in both directions between any two class positions.

When we review the sociological literature, we find much more use being made of odds ratios than of disparity ratios, even though they are much more difficult to interpret substantively (Adam Swift does his best: 'Odds ratios measure the statistical probability of members of one sub-group having some characteristic and not having another, relative to the statistical probability of another group having and not having those same characteristics.')[9] Odds ratios are calculated mainly for the purposes of statistical modelling, or to compare 'overall fluidity' rates over time, or across different societies, but standing alone as descriptive statistics, they are not particularly illuminating.

This has not, however, stopped researchers from appealing to the size of an odds ratio to support a substantive claim of unfairness and class privilege. In his 1972 survey, for example, Goldthorpe calculated odds ratios for different birth cohorts of service class and working class men ranging between 13 and 19, and when he focused on the furthest extremes, comparing the top of the service class (class I, the higher level professional, managerial and administrative jobs together with large proprietors) with the bottom of the working class (class VII, the semi- and unskilled manual workers), he ended up with odds ratios as high as 36. At various points in his book, Goldthorpe refers to such figures as 'gross',[10] and he appeals to them to support his claim that, 'The reality of contemporary British society most strikingly and incontrovertibly deviates from the ideal of genuine openness.'[11]

Later studies have followed Goldthorpe's example. In their analysis of mobility rates based on the UK general election surveys, for example, Heath and Payne reported that 46 per cent of class I men stayed in class I, while six per cent fell all the way to class VII. Against this, only nine per cent of class VII men ended up in class I while 38 per cent stayed put. This produces an odds ratio of 33:1. They conclude: 'The odds ratios would all be 1 in a society where social origins were unrelated to class destinations. The larger the odds ratio, the more unequal the competition, and the ratio of 33:1 suggests that the competition is extremely unequal.'[12]

In fact, it tells us no such thing. It does not follow from the fact that mobility outcomes are unequal that the competition was unequal— even though generations of sociologists have jumped to precisely this conclusion. We have to ask *why* different people achieve different outcomes relative to each other—we cannot simply deduce from the existence of an odds ratio greater than 1 that there must be some sort of unfair privilege or blockage at work. This is a crucial issue and is one we shall address in more detail later in this book.

The problem with odds ratios

Odds ratios combine success and failure chances in a single statistic. A significant narrowing of odds ratios therefore requires, not only that working class chances improve, but also that middle class chances deteriorate—there needs to be a 'levelling down' as well as a 'levelling up'.

Trevor Noble points out that, with an expanding middle class and a contracting working class, it is unlikely that this will occur, so odds ratios will almost certainly fail to register the improvements that have occurred in mobility opportunities over time.[13] Faced with an expansion of middle class positions, it would be extraordinary if middle class parents did not take as much advantage of the new opportunities available as working class parents did. As Noble puts it: 'It is hard to imagine, given the economic, cultural, motivational and other advantages attributed to a middle class upbringing, in what circum-

---

stances widening opportunities to pursue an interesting and well-paid career would not also be at least equally available to middle class children as well as any others.'[14]

Furthermore, with 'less room at the bottom', there is less and less chance that people who are already at the top will fall to the bottom. We should, therefore, *expect* the improved rates of upward mobility witnessed during the twentieth century to be accompanied by a corresponding decline in rates of downward mobility. But this means odds ratios will remain more-or-less constant, even though opportunities have been expanding.

Breen and Goldthorpe are irritated by arguments like this. They claim that 'with a modicum of sociological imagination' it is possible to conceive of odds ratios falling even in situations where the middle class is expanding. If barriers to working class achievement were 'to some degree reduced', they say, then talented working class children will take advantage of any expansion in middle class jobs faster than dull middle class children do, in which case odds ratios will fall.[15]

But Breen and Goldthorpe are wrong. Even if working class children seize the lion's share of the new opportunities, there is no reason to believe that odds ratios will fall. Consider a society of one thousand individuals divided into just two classes, with three-quarters of them in the working class, and assume that the shape of the class system does not change from generation to generation. Twenty per cent of middle class children (50 in all) fall into the working class in each generation, but this only creates room for seven per cent of working class children (50 in all) to move up, for the working class is so much larger than the middle class. Measuring 'social fluidity' in this society, we end up with an odds ratio of 56 (Phase A).

Now imagine, as Breen and Goldthorpe suggest, that policies are introduced to improve working class mobility chances 'to some degree'. Indeed, allow these policies to be so successful that the number of working class children moving into the middle class doubles, from 50 to 100. This, of course, will require that more middle class children move down (for the number of top positions remains constant), so 40 per cent of middle class children (100 out of 250) are now downwardly mobile. The odds ratio improves considerably, to 9.75 (Phase B1).

But now add Trevor Noble's scenario. The same successful social reforms are introduced, but at the same time, the occupational system starts changing (Phase B2). Not only do 50 additional working class children displace 50 children from the middle class, but the number of middle class positions expands (say, from 250 to 400).

So committed are reformers to improving 'social fluidity' that they take advice from Breen and Goldthorpe who tell them odds ratios will improve if 'there is a more rapid improvement in the chances of upward mobility of working class children than of children of more advantaged backgrounds'. Of the 150 new middle class jobs, therefore, no fewer than 100 are reserved for working class children and only 50 go to middle class children. While middle class children's chances of a middle class position improve by 25 per cent (from 150 to 200), the equivalent chances of working class children improve by 100 per cent (from 100 to 200), amply meeting Breen and Goldthorpe's requirement.

The new odds ratio is then calculated but reformers are dismayed to find that it has now *risen* to 11. Despite the fact that the same positive discrimination programme has been introduced as in Phase B1, things have apparently got 'worse' in Phase B2 simply because the size of the middle class has increased. This is despite the fact that the number of working class children experiencing upward mobility has doubled as compared with Phase B1, and twice as many of the newly created middle class positions have gone to working class children than to middle class children. Social fluidity has nevertheless 'deteriorated' according to the odds ratios because middle class downward mobility rates have eased with the increasing size of that class. This is precisely the problem identified in Trevor Noble's work.

This problem is not limited to hypothetical examples—it occurs in reality. Goldthorpe's own research on his 1972 and 1983 samples showed that, relative to middle class children, the chances of working class children achieving a middle class job shortened 4:1 to 3:1. At the same time, however, the chances of middle class children ending up in the working class (compared with those of working class children) lengthened from 4:1 to 5:1. Breen and Goldthorpe interpret these changes by insisting that fluidity in this period was *'unchanged'* because 'relative rates, as measured by odds ratios, were not significantly different in the mobility tables for the two dates'.[16] But this blinds them to the crucial fact that more working class children 'gained' even though fewer middle class children 'lost'. The odds ratio fails to pick this up because opportunity opened up for one class at the same time as threats were reduced to the other.

Breen and Goldthorpe maintain that the strength of odds ratios is that they are 'insensitive to the marginal distributions of mobility tables' (a point which they rather patronisingly claim I 'fail to grasp'). Arguably, however, this is precisely their weakness, for by failing to take account of changes in the marginal totals in mobility tables (i.e. in the size of the classes from and to which people are moving), odds ratios treat social mobility as if it were a zero-sum game. The rules of measurement ensure that nobody can win unless somebody else loses, which is precisely what Noble is attacking when he suggests that 'pure mobility' cannot in any meaningful way be partialled out from 'structural mobility'.

All of this has profound implications for public policy debates (discussed in chapter VII). A policy of improving opportunities for talented individuals from all classes to realize their full potential need not require us to force more middle class children to fail. We do not have to reduce odds ratios to unity (as Goldthorpe suggests); we need only reduce to unity the disparity ratio measuring working class and middle class children's chances of achieving a middle class position (once differences of ability and effort have been taken into account). If we measure success by changes in odds ratios, however, we shall have to ensure that the children of the middle classes are made to suffer at the same time as the children of the working classes gain. But in reality, in a fair society, both can gain. Indeed, both have been gaining over a period of many years.

Table 4 shows the odds ratios (calculated by Goldthorpe and Jackson)[17] for men's and women's mobility chances in the two national birth cohort studies. Mobility for the 1958 cohort (NCDS) is assessed when they were aged 33, while that for the 1970 cohort (BCS) is assessed at age 30. More mobility will, of course, have occurred since then, for we noted earlier that intra-generational mobility is common and continues throughout people's working lives, but by their early thirties, we have a reasonably good idea of the trajectory on which many people are set.

Table 4
Symmetrical odds ratios for service class (Class I & II) and working class
(Class VI & VII) origins and destinations in the 1958 (upper figures)
and 1970 (lower figures) birth cohort studies

Men:

	Class II*	Class VI	Class VII
Class I	1.5	7.5	13.8
	1.6	10.3	21.8
Class II*		2.8	9.6
		3.0	5.3
Class VI			1.3
			1.6

Women:

	Class II*	Class VI	Class VII**
Class I	1.2	2.9	5.9
	1.4	10.9	11.0
Class II*		2.3	4.8
		4.0	3.6
Class VI			0.6
			1.2

* Includes Class IVa (self-employed with employees)
** Includes Class IIIb (personal service workers)

Several points can be noted from this table. The tiny odds ratios for classes I and II in both surveys, and for both sexes, tell us that movement between the higher and lower levels of the service class is readily possible for both men and women. There are clearly no barriers of any sort here. Similarly, classes VI and VII (the skilled versus semi- and unskilled working class) appear to be very open to each other (odds ratios no higher than 1.6). More interestingly, the odds ratios for classes II (lower service class) and VI (skilled manual workers) are also surprisingly small (below 3 for both men and women in the 1958 cohort), which suggests there is also extensive interchange (down as well as up) between these two positions, even though they are located at opposite ends of the system. It is only really the extreme ends—the upper service class and the semi- and unskilled manual working class— which throw up large odds ratios when they are compared with each

31

other (ranging from 6 for women in the 1958 cohort, to 22 for men in the 1970 birth cohort).

Even here, though, the figures are not as large as were reported in the earlier surveys. Does this indicate that the class system has been getting more fluid over the last 40 years or so?

Do relative mobility rates increase over time?

In his work with Erikson, Goldthorpe famously argued that overall 'fluidity' (as measured by odds ratios) has tended to remain fairly constant over time. He found this was true, not only in Britain, but in almost all western countries, and he referred to this pattern as 'trendless fluctuation', or a 'constant flux'.[18] He appealed to this finding to challenge theorists of modernisation who have long believed that as societies industrialise, and their markets free up, so individual opportunities open up too. Goldthorpe suggests this is not the case, and that although absolute mobility has expanded, class privileges and disadvantages continue to make themselves felt in relative rates which remain fairly constant.

There are, however, grounds for doubting this claim. In their analysis of election samples, Heath and Payne calculate a series of odds ratios for different birth cohorts, and they find they have been falling (Table 5). For men and women born before the Second World War, odds ratios expressing movement between the service class and the working class are significantly higher than for those born later. Heath and Payne test this apparent change with a series of statistical models which oblige them to reject the hypothesis of constant fluidity for men, although the result for women is less certain. In plain English: the odds ratios have been getting smaller, which indicates (certainly for men, and possibly for women) that fluidity has been increasing.

Table 5
Odds ratios (service class: working class) for men and women
born in the first 60 years of the twentieth century

	Pre 1900	1900	1910	1920	1930	1940	1950-59
Men:	16.0	10.0	19.0	14.0	10.3	5.6	7.7
Women:	Na	17.2	15.2	13.4	7.3	10.6	5.8

Other studies confirm this. Analysing the British Household Panel Study, and looking at people's occupations by the time they reached 35 years of age, Gershuny reports consistently falling odds ratios (based on service class/working class comparisons) for generations born after 1940.[19] He speculates that Goldthorpe may have failed to spot this trend because he analysed later cohorts when they were younger than the older ones, which means he could have missed later career movements.

Drawing on a unique family history data set from the nineteenth century, which they link to more recent survey data, Lambert and his colleagues also find that 'fluidity' has been increasing over time in Britain, albeit very slowly: 'We can see remarkably consistent patterns of trend in social mobility rates over the last two hundred years. The trend of slowly increasing social mobility is particularly stable for men, and is also clear, though less stable, for women.'[20] They define people's class as a point on a continuous, hierarchical scale, and this enables them to estimate the strength of the association between fathers' and sons' occupations using correlation coefficients. They find the strength of correlations has been declining over time, and they note with some alarm the readiness of UK policy makers to accept Goldthorpe's 'constant fluidity' model when it appears to be wrong.

This is not the only example we shall encounter of politicians and government advisers developing policies on the basis of faulty assumptions about social mobility patterns.

3

Is Social Mobility Falling?

Given the conclusion of the previous chapter, the title of this one needs some justification. Why would anybody believe that social mobility is falling when we have already established that it has been expanding for about two hundred years?

The answer lies in the recent, very influential, work of a group of economists who have been looking at income mobility, comparing the 1958 and 1970 national birth cohort studies. They think they have found a clear reduction in the rate of mobility between these two cohorts. Children born in 1970 are said to be facing greater obstacles to success than those born just twelve years earlier. This claim has sent shock waves through the political system, sparking enquiries, parliamentary debates and a spate of policy initiatives intended to sponsor more working class achievement while weakening the tenacious grip on success of the children of the bourgeoisie.

Income mobility in the 1958 birth cohort

To evaluate these economists' claims, we need to understand that they are analysing a different phenomenon from the one we have been looking at until now. The sociological literature we have reviewed in the last two chapters is concerned with *class mobility*, whereas the economists are looking at *income mobility*.

Class mobility versus income mobility

Sociologists prefer to analyse movement between classes because, although definitions of 'class' are disputed, and its measurement is inexact, the idea of 'class' captures a much broader sense of people's 'life chances' than simply income. Whether you call them the 'service class', the 'salariat', or the 'middle class', highly-qualified professionals, together with top managers and administrators and successful entre- preneurs, share a number of material circumstances in common which tend to separate them quite sharply from the manual 'working class'. They tend to earn more, but they also enjoy greater security of employ- ment, they tend to have better retirement pensions (although

---

nowadays, this increasingly depends on public sector employment), they are generally better educated, they have a 'cultural capital' as well as economic assets which they can pass onto their children, they enjoy better lifetime health, they tend to be more highly-regarded in the community (and they have higher self-esteem too), and they exercise more control over their own work lives, and the lives of those they employ or manage.

Class, moreover, tends to be more enduring than mere income. Income can be ephemeral—ask what somebody is earning today, and it could be quite different this time next year. Class too, of course, can and does change (we have seen that intra-generational mobility is common), but it offers a more reliable indicator of somebody's long-term life prospects than one or two simple snapshots of their income can provide.[1]

Economists, on the other hand, prefer to work with income data. Income is, in principle, more easily measured (although you have to trust that people are telling you the truth about what they earn), and there are fewer doctrinal debates about how to define it (although it can be difficult knowing what to include, and calculating net incomes after receipt of benefits and payment of tax can be problematic when relying on survey answers). It is a simple indicator of people's wellbeing, and (unlike 'class') everybody understands what you are talking about.

There are also methodological advantages. Because you are dealing with real numbers, you can use much stronger statistical tools to analyse income data. And you don't encounter the clunking problem (which sociologists have never very satisfactorily resolved) of how to classify households where one member of a couple occupies a higher class than the other (this is becoming a major problem in research on social mobility as more women have careers; which parent's job is to be used to determine a child's class of origin when both are in full-time employment but occupy different class positions?). If you are using income data, this problem can be sidestepped: simply add the parental incomes together.

One important implication of the economists' decision to study income rather than class mobility is that the concept of 'absolute' mobility disappears in this tradition of work. This is because movement takes place between different income bands (usually quartiles) so the marginal totals are fixed in advance. There is a one in four chance of ending up in any given quartile, and this remains the case no matter how much the income distribution might change over time. The middle class may get bigger as the working class shrinks, but income quartiles remain proportionately the same size for ever.[2]

Early work by economists analysing income mobility in the 1958 birth cohort produced results broadly comparable to those produced by sociologists on relative class mobility. Dividing the sample into income deciles, Institute for Fiscal Studies researchers showed that, by age 33, men in the top tenth of earnings had fathers drawn from right across the income range.[3] Nevertheless, there was a clear relationship between fathers' and sons' incomes: 21 per cent of the fathers of men in the top decile were themselves also in the top decile (twice as many as would be expected by chance), while only five per cent of them were in the bottom decile (half as many as there should have been if incomes of parents and their children were not linked). This equates to a disparity ratio of around 4:1.

When economists tried to estimate the strength of this association between parents' and children's incomes, they found very weak correlations (r=0.24 for sons and r=0.35 for daughters). However, some of them suspected this was because parents' incomes were being measured at just one point in time, so the estimates they were getting were skewed by transitory fluctuations. They tried to adjust for this by estimating parents' long-term earnings from other information collected about them at other sweeps of the survey, and after making these adjustments, they came up with much stronger correlations of between 0.4 and 0.6. They concluded: 'We are confident that the extent of mobility is very limited in terms of earnings', although they did concede that upward mobility (among those born to parents at the bottom of the income distribution) was not uncommon. As with class mobility, so too with incomes, most of the 'stickiness' was due to the relatively low probability of those born to the richest parents ending up poor.[4]

A note on measuring correlation

Statisticians commonly measure the strength of association between two (interval) variables by using a statistic known as *Pearson's Product Moment Correlation Coefficient*, whose symbol is r. The Pearson correlation coefficient is a number between -1 and +1 (a negative value indicates that the relationship is inverse—i.e. as the value of one variable increases, the value of the other decreases). The stronger the association, the higher the value of the coefficient (a value of 0 therefore indicates complete absence of association, while +1 or -1 indicates that one completely predicts the other). Correlations less than plus or minus 0.3 are generally regarded as quite weak.

It is important to remember that correlation does not prove causation. Two variables may be correlated without one influencing the other (e.g. they might both be causally linked to a common third variable).

The 'falling rate' of income mobility

The picture became a lot gloomier when income data from the 1970 birth cohort study became available. In 2005, the Sutton Trust funded and published a report by three economists, Jo Blanden, Paul Gregg and Stephen Machin, who claimed that intergenerational income mobility rates were lower in the UK than in Canada, Scandinavia and (probably) Germany, and that Britain was the only country where rates were falling.[5] They linked this fall to evidence that the expansion of higher education in Britain had benefited richer children more than poorer ones. Because the children of affluent parents were taking disproportionate advantage of the higher number of university places, they were grabbing the best jobs in ever greater numbers.

Together with Lindsey MacMillan, these researchers have elaborated their findings in a series of later papers, all of which rest on the key claim that income mobility is lower in the 1970 birth cohort (BCS) than in the 1958 cohort (NCDS).[6]

This claim was established in their original report by comparing mobility rates for men in their early thirties (33 for the NCDS sample, and 30 in BCS)—although fewer than half the men in each survey were included in the analysis due to inadequate income data for themselves or their parents. Mobility was assessed by comparing the income quartile to which their parents belonged when these men were aged 16 (their mothers' and fathers' incomes were combined and then averaged) with the income quartile to which they themselves belonged by the age of 33/30. The results are summarised in Table 6.

Table 6
Income mobility in the 1958 (upper figures) and
1970 (lower figures) birth cohort studies

	Sons' earning quartile (age 33/30)			
Parental income quartile	Bottom	Second	Third	Top
Bottom	.31	.28	.23	.17
	.38	.25	.21	.16
Second	.30	.28	.23	.19
	.29	.28	.26	.17
Third	.22	.25	.25	.28
	.22	.26	.28	.25
Top	.17	.20	.28	.35
	.11	.22	.24	.42

The first thing to say about Table 6 is that these figures are not very large. 'Perfect mobility' (with no association between your parent's income and what you earn) would be represented by .25 in every cell (for one quarter of the children from each parental income group would end up in each quarter of the income distribution). Look at the figures for the second and third quartiles of sons' earnings, and that is more-or-less what was found. It seems that 'middle income earners' are recruited from origins right across the income distribution.

It is at the top and the bottom that destinations become more closely associated with origins. Children born into the lowest quartile are significantly under-represented (0.16 and 0.17) at the top, and those born into the top quartile are quite heavily under-represented at the bottom (0.17 and 0.11). Poorer children are therefore less successful than the law of averages would lead us to expect, and richer children are more adept at avoiding downward mobility than would be expected by chance. These results are broadly consistent with what sociologists have reported for class mobility.

What got Blanden and her fellow economists excited, however, was that these patterns are clearly more pronounced in the 1970 than the 1958 cohort. Looking at the NCDS sons from the top quartile, 35 per cent got to the top band themselves, while only 17 per cent ended up at the bottom. In the BCS, however, 42 per cent made it to the top, and just 11 per cent wound up at the bottom. Here, then, is the evidence of declining mobility, which the authors immediately equated with a 'decline in equality of opportunity'.[7]

That there is a significant difference in rates of income mobility between the cohorts is demonstrated by two different statistics measuring the association between parental income and sons' income in the two samples. The 'coefficient of elasticity' (designated by the Greek letter β, or Beta), which basically measures the amount by which sons' incomes change as parental incomes change, rose from 0.205 in NCDS to 0.291 in BCS; the correlation coefficient (r), which expresses the strength of association between parents' and sons' incomes, rose from 0.166 in NCDS to 0.286 in BCS.[8] The differences between both sets of coefficients (β and r) are sizeable, and they are statistically significant. The finding therefore appeared to be robust: income mobility declined for those born in 1970 compared with those born 12 years earlier.

Explaining the 'fall' in income mobility

Various explanations have been offered for why children born in 1970 appear to be encountering more obstacles than those born in 1958. Former Labour minister David Blunkett thinks it may reflect a difference of labour market conditions when they left school, but it is difficult to accept that the BCS cohort leaving school in the mid-1980s faced worse conditions than the NCDS children trying to build careers in the economic stagflation of the mid-1970s.[9] Others believe 'progressive' education reforms designed to reduce class privileges may, paradoxically, have had precisely the opposite effect: 'By removing "elitist" ability related selection mechanisms in the system, such as grammar schools and streaming students by ability, we have actually enabled parental social class to become a more important determinant of success.'[10]

Some people think changes in patterns of childhood behaviour may be implicated. Psychological indicators like anxiety, self-esteem, hyper-activity and locus of control all correlate to some extent with future income, and their association with parental income is somewhat stronger in the 1970 study than in the 1958 one. In other words, parents' income became more strongly associated with how people behaved as children, and this in turn helps predict their income in adulthood.[11]

Interestingly, however, the link between cognitive ability (reading and maths scores and IQ at age 11) and later income weakens as between the 1958 and 1970 cohorts, although it remains quite strong in both (we shall consider the significance of ability in shaping economic success in later chapters). This lends support to the most popular explanation for the apparent fall in mobility, which is that low ability children from the middle class started going to university in greater numbers, which allowed them to achieve more economic success than before.

What allowed this to happen was the expansion of higher education in the 1980s and 1990s. Conservative MP, David Willetts, has drawn attention to the way the expansion of higher education particularly enabled more middle class girls to go to university (university entrance by girls from low-income families stayed constant at just six per cent in both the 1958 and 1970 cohorts, but girls born into richer households increased their participation from 21 per cent to 36 per cent). He thinks this may explain the fall in income mobility rates between the two studies, for not only did it inflate the proportion of middle class children in higher education, but it also increased 'assortive mating' (i.e. many of these graduate women ended up partnering graduate men). As Willetts puts it, 'If advantage marries advantage then we must not be surprised if social mobility suffers... increasing equality between the sexes has meant increasing inequality between social classes. Feminism has trumped egalitarianism.'[12]

But it was not just middle class girls who benefited. The opportunities opened up by the expansion of the universities allowed less able children of more affluent families to go into higher education in increasing numbers, whatever their sex. By the time the NCDS children reached age 23 (in 1981), 20 per cent of those from the richest quintile of families had a degree, compared with just six per cent of those from the poorest quintile. But when the BCS children reached the same age, just 12 years later, 37 per cent of those from the richest families had degrees (almost double the NCDS figure), while the proportion from poorer families had barely altered (up just one percentage point to seven per cent). And this trend seems to have continued, for by 1999, 46 per cent of the richest children from the BHPS had degrees compared with just nine per cent from the poorest quintile.[13]

As the parental income effect on participation in higher education strengthened over these years, so the association with IQ scores weakened. This is because the new places available in universities went, in roughly equal proportions, to the bright children of low income parents and to the dull children of high income parents.[14] Even allowing for class differences in intelligence, affluent children therefore went to university following the expansion in disproportionate numbers. It is claimed that this helps explain the stronger correlation between parental income and their own income in the later birth cohort.[15]

What is happening to later cohorts?

Assuming that increasing inequality of access to higher education, coupled with an increase in behavioural problems among working class children, are the factors that drove the decline in income mobility from the 1958 to the 1970 cohorts, Blanden and Machin look at how these early predictors of economic success or failure have been panning out for children born more recently.[16] From this, they try to predict the likely income mobility patterns for generations that have not yet become established in the labour force.

For their subjects, they draw on (a) children born in the 1990s to members of the British Household Panel Study, (b) children born to members of the 1958 and 1970 cohort studies, and (c) the new 'Millenium' cohort study, which is following a sample of children born in 2000. They find for all these groups that the association between parental income and behavioural problems in childhood, reading score at age 11, and (for those who are old enough) getting a degree by age 23, has not strengthened relative to the equivalent correlations recorded in the 1970 cohort. They conclude: 'These results suggest that we might expect to observe little change in intergenerational income mobility for the cohorts born from around 1970 onwards.'[17]

Not surprisingly, government ministers have seized on this (extremely tentative) finding to suggest that their policies have halted the 'decline' in social mobility, and may even be reversing it.[18] In reality, of course, we do not know whether later cohorts will be more or less mobile than the 1970 sample, because they haven't even left school yet.

How could income mobility have fallen when class mobility remained constant?

There is, however, a problem with all of these explanations for the decline in *income mobility* between the 1958 and 1970 cohorts, which is that *class mobility* shows no sign of having fallen. Given the strong association between income and social class, this makes little sense.[19] If the expansion of higher education explains why children from affluent families became more successful in improving their income, why hasn't this also shown up in their class destinations? Similarly, if growing behavioural difficulties blighted the chances of poorer children achieving a high income, shouldn't this also show up in a lower rate of upward mobility for lower class children?

Sociologists researching class mobility and using exactly the same two data sets (the 1958 and 1970 cohorts) have found no sign of the decline in mobility rates which has so agitated the economists (and, following them, the politicians). In 2007, Goldthorpe and Jackson published a paper analysing class mobility of NCDS members at age 33 and BCS members at age 30 (i.e. exactly the same comparison as that used in the Sutton Trust report).[20] They divided the samples into men and women (the economists' findings deal only with men) and analysed both absolute and relative mobility trends (as explained earlier, the economists' findings can deal only with relative mobility). They found no significant change in any of these categories.

Looking first at absolute mobility rates, Goldthorpe and Jackson reported 'negligible' change for women, and almost no overall change for men, although downward mobility for males has increased slightly (from 27 per cent in NCDS to 30 per cent in BCS) while upward mobility has decreased a bit (from 45 per cent in NCDS to 42 per cent in BCS). They suggest that, for men, the long period of middle class expansion, which drove much of the increased social mobility of the twentieth century, may at last be slowing as the expansion of public sector employment slows and as competition from women intensifies. This is politically significant, as we shall see in chapter 7, but the key point for our present purposes is that there has been no change in overall male mobility (the slight fall in upward movement is cancelled out by the slight increase in downward movement).

They then looked at relative mobility rates, calculating the series of odds ratios already presented in Table 4 (p. 31). The conclusion is the same. Applying a series of best-fitting models, they find no general tendency for fluidity to rise or fall. They describe as their 'main and most securely grounded result' the finding that 'the pattern of fluidity underlying the two cohort mobility tables that we have constructed is very much the same'.[21]

The following year, Goldthorpe (in a paper with Colin Mills) attempted to estimate absolute and relative mobility rates in Britain between 1972 and 2005.[22] In addition to the two birth cohort studies, they drew upon data from the government's General Household Survey, various election surveys, and the EU Income and Living Conditions survey of 2005.

They concluded that absolute mobility for men had (as Goldthorpe suspected) flattened out due to the slowdown in the expansion of the middle class and increased competition from women for the best jobs. Absolute mobility for women was still increasing, with more upward and less downward movement (which used to be the pattern for men in the earlier part of the last century). But for men, movement up and down was unchanged since the 1980s.

As regards relative mobility, however, there had been no change for men or women. If anything, fluidity for males might have eased a bit, but it certainly had not tightened. There was no support for the economists' claim that relative mobility was in decline, and Goldthorpe and Mills were uncompromising in challenging it: 'In political circles, and in turn in the media, it seems widely believed that in recent decades intergenerational social mobility in Britain has declined—even in fact "ground to a halt"... our results reveal that this prevailing view is simply mistaken... In sum, while there are no strong grounds for regarding Britain today as being a more mobile society than it was in the 1970s, nor the British class structure as being more "open", there are no grounds at all for taking the opposite view.'[23]

Has income mobility really fallen?

Part of the explanation for the divergence in findings between the sociologists and the economists may lie in the increased rate of employment of women. More of the mothers of the 1970 cohort were earning an income than had been the case in the 1958 cohort. This is significant because the Sutton Trust report derived its estimates of income mobility in both cohorts by comparing sons' earnings with the *combined* earnings of both of their parents (the BCS only records total household income of fathers and mothers combined, so to ensure comparability, they combined the fathers' and mothers' incomes in the NCDS sample too). Sociologists, on the other hand, assess the class background of cohort members on the basis of only one parent's occupation, usually the father's.[24]

The problem with subsuming two employed parents under one social class category is that they are often doing very different kinds of jobs. Blanden and her fellow researchers show that fathers' incomes correlate very poorly with mothers' incomes. When they focused solely on families where only the father worked, they found the fall in mobility rates between the 1958 and 1970 cohorts looked smaller than when they included both parents' incomes.[25] They concluded from this that one reason why sociologists have failed to pick up on declining mobility may be that they have been ignoring the growing importance of maternal employment when measuring children's socio-economic background: 'Women's labour market participation and single mother-hood mean that mothers' incomes are increasingly essential to children's economic wellbeing.'[26]

Erikson and Goldthorpe, however, offer a different explanation. They think the problem lies in the reliability of the data used by the economists to calculate family income for the 1958 cohort.[27] What is odd, according to them, is not the stronger association between parental and children's incomes in the later panel (BCS), but the unexpectedly weak association between them in the earlier one (NCDS). The (unadjusted) correlation between family earnings and child's earnings in the NCDS sample is just 0.18 for sons, and 0.16 for daughters. This is very weak—much weaker than the correlation between fathers' class and children's class—and Erikson and Goldthorpe think it points to something wrong with the (derived) 'family income variable' in the 1958 data set.

They back up their suspicions by showing that the strength of association between parents and children on a range of other, related variables remained constant as between the two cohorts. Not only does the correlation between father's class and child's class remain more-or-less unchanged, but so too does that between father's class and child's earnings, and between child's class and child's earnings. Yet the correlations between these different variables and the family income variable all strengthen markedly between the two cohorts. All of this suggests that the derived family income variable in NCDS is an unreliable measure, and that the decreased income mobility recorded by the Sutton Trust economists has been caused by error in the estimation of family incomes in the 1958 cohort.

The suspicion that income mobility in the earlier study is over-estimated is further supported by the Sutton Trust team's claims regarding access to higher education. They believe that the reduced income mobility they found can be explained partly by an increased association between family income and university attendance, and Erikson and Goldthorpe agree that this association does indeed strengthen between the two cohorts. However, Erikson and Goldthorpe go on to show that this finding is almost certainly due to the unreliability of the family income variable computed for the 1958 cohort, for other relevant associations linked to participation in higher education do not change.

Additional grounds for doubting the reliability of the Sutton Trust findings come from an analysis of income mobility based on the British Household Panel Survey (BHPS) looking at cohorts of men born in the period 1950 to 1972.[28] The authors find no change in income mobility rates over this period. While they do detect a slight strengthening in the elasticity coefficient (indicating a reduction in intergenerational mobility) for children born in the 1961-72 period (which roughly corresponds to the BCS 1970 birth cohort), this seems to be due to the increasing variance in incomes, and it disappears when the association between fathers' and sons' incomes is measured by correlation coefficients. The authors conclude: 'There are no strong changes in intergenerational mobility across cohorts from 1950 to 1972.'[29]

What could have gone wrong in the computation of family income for the 1958 birth cohort? One obvious possibility is that errors have crept in while creating the derived variable.[30] Another possibility, favoured by Erikson and Goldthorpe (but denied by Blanden and her team),[31] is that family incomes in the earlier cohort varied much more than in the later cohort (national data for the relevant periods show that transitory fluctuations in male earnings were significantly greater). This means any estimate of family income based on a single snapshot of earnings at one time will carry a greater risk of error (we saw earlier that economists themselves were worried about this when they first analysed the NCDS parental data in the mid-1990s). Parental incomes in both studies were recorded when the children reached 16. For the NCDS children, this was in 1974, at the height of the chaos surrounding the miners' strike, the three-day week and rapidly-spiralling wage inflation. Adjustments to parental income data were made at the time by NCDS researchers to try to take account of these unusual circumstances, but it would not be surprising if the data contained an unusually high amount of error.[32]

Whatever the explanation, the conclusion seems clear: the fall in income mobility recorded by the Sutton Trust report, to which so much political attention has been paid, is almost certainly a statistical artefact. Either it did not happen, or if it did, the shift was tiny. As David Goodhart (editor of *Prospect*), complains: 'This slender analysis has, arguably, had more influence on public policy debate than any other academic paper of the last 20 years... the lazy consensus which has decreed the end of social mobility is both wrong and damaging.'[33]

4

What Would a Perfect Meritocracy Look Like?

We have seen (Table 3, p. 25) that middle class children are two or three times more likely than working class children to end up in middle class jobs. Likewise, working class children are three or four times more likely to end up in working class jobs. So what do these 'disparity ratios' tell us about opportunities in modern Britain?

The fallacy of deducing causes from outcomes

Generally, sociologists have assumed that unequal outcomes like these signify unfair selection procedures. The fact that middle class children are more successful on average than working class children is assumed to 'prove' that the system is working unfairly, that 'social advantage and disadvantage' is helping middle class children and blocking working class children, and that meritocracy is no more than a myth.

But there is another possibility. What if middle class children are on average brighter than working class children, or if they work harder on average than their working class peers? Under meritocratic conditions, we would then *expect* the children of the middle classes to fare better in the competition for educational and occupational success, for a meritocracy is precisely a system which allocates positions on the basis of ability and effort.

This possibility that 'merit' (ability and motivation) is unevenly distributed across social classes has generally been ruled out by sociologists as a result of the way they have interpreted their measures of relative social mobility rates. Whether they focus on disparity ratios or odds ratios, their criterion of social justice or fairness is a ratio of 1:1. A fair and open society is defined as one where all children, regardless of social origins, have exactly the same *statistical* chance of ending up in any given position. Any ratio in excess of 1:1—i.e. any evidence that class destinations are not randomly distributed in comparison with class origins—is taken as evidence that the society is treating children from different class origins unfairly.

Take, for example, John Goldthorpe's 1972 mobility survey. He found odds ratios (at the extremes of the class system) as high as 30:1, and he concluded from this that: 'The reality of contemporary British society most strikingly and incontrovertibly deviates from the ideal of genuine openness.'[1] But this claim was based entirely on his disparity ratios and odds ratios. Anything in excess of 1:1 was assumed to indicate the existence of social barriers blocking working class children from rising and safeguarding middle class children from falling. No attempt was made to investigate what these barriers might be—he just 'knew' they existed from the fact that the disparity and odds ratios were so high.

The same logic was followed by the Essex University team in the 1980s. Reporting service class:working class odds ratios of 7:1 (for men) and 13:1 (for women), they too concluded: 'The post-war project of creating in Britain a more open society... has signally failed to secure its objective.'[2] Like Goldthorpe, they felt no need to investigate what had produced these outcomes. Rather, they reasoned backwards, from the fact of unequal mobility chances to the implied existence of unfair class competition that 'must' have generated them.

The same kind of fallacious reasoning is still widespread today, only now it is cropping up in the pronouncements of politicians and government bureaucrats as well as in academic research reports:

- A 2001 Cabinet Office review of the evidence on social mobility suggests that a meritocratic society should be marked by 'the absence of any association between class origins and destinations'.[3] Anything greater than a 1:1 disparity ratio is assumed to demonstrate the existence of class barriers.

- The 2008, *Getting On, Getting Ahead* report, prepared for Labour Prime Minister Gordon Brown, defines 'perfect mobility' as the absence of any statistical association between origins and destinations and sees 'large and systematic differences in outcomes' as evidence against meritocratic selection.[4]

- The 2010 National Equality Panel report appeals to 'the systematic nature of many of the differences' to deny the possibility of 'equality of opportunity' between the classes.[5]

- The Conservatives, too, now see unequal outcomes as evidence of unequal opportunities. In a recent parliamentary debate Conservative spokesperson, David Willetts, deduced from the fact that children from rich neighbourhoods go to university in greater numbers than children from poor neighbourhoods that, 'There are still enormous gaps in the opportunities for young people to go to university.'[6] Again, disparity in outcomes is assumed to signify inequality of opportunity.

All these reports may be right, of course. It may be that children from poorer backgrounds are being unfairly denied opportunities, and that this explains why they perform worse on average than children from more affluent backgrounds. But it may also be that, on average, they are not as bright. This latter possibility may be politically unpalatable—perhaps even unmentionable in a democratic age—but it is misleading and dishonest for academics and politicians simply to assume that any evidence that children from different social class backgrounds perform differently is proof of unequal opportunities between them.

Evidence on relative social mobility rates can of itself tell us nothing about the fairness or unfairness of the society in which we live. There are two different explanations that could account for it: the SAD thesis is one, and the meritocracy thesis is the other. To judge which is correct (or which is stronger), we need to start looking at evidence to see whether unequal outcomes are due to unfair competition or to an unequal distribution of talents and capacities. We need, in other words, to investigate *why* children from certain kinds of backgrounds perform better than those from others. And this means taking intelligence seriously.

Cognitive ability: the missing variable in social mobility research

To insist (as Goldthorpe and the Cabinet Office do) that in a 'genuinely open' society, there should be *no* association between class origins and class destinations (i.e. that meritocracy requires disparity ratios of 1:1), we have to assume one of two things is true:

- Either, employers select individuals randomly without regard for any differences of talent and ability between them;

- Or the pool of talented and able individuals is spread equally and randomly across the class system.

The first possibility is clearly absurd. We do not expect employers to take on the first individual who walks through the door, irrespective of his or her individual qualities. Occupational recruitment is and must be selective.[7]

But if occupational recruitment is necessarily selective by ability, then a 1:1 disparity ratio between two generations can only come about if ability (and effort) are spread evenly across all social classes. This in turn requires, not only that intelligence is randomly distributed, but also that there are *no* differences of intelligence that can be passed on from parents to their children. This too is absurd.

Just think it through for a moment. Given that people are recruited to occupations to some extent on the basis of their ability, then in any one generation we should find people of higher ability occupying the higher social class positions. If differences of ability are at all innate, this will in turn mean that the children born to these parents will tend to inherit some of their parents' intellectual strengths. The result will be that average ability levels will then vary between children from different social class backgrounds as well as their parents.

This logic is compelling, but it has been anathema to sociologists who, for most of the last fifty years, have been analysing social mobility rates while persistently ignoring the question of differences of intelligence between the classes.[8] In his book of well over 300 pages, for example, John Goldthorpe took just one paragraph to dispense with the possibility that the pattern of social mobility he had found could be explained by social class differences in average levels of intelligence (he dismissed the idea as 'social Darwinist' and 'Smilesian').[9]

By dismissing intelligence-based theories of social mobility so casually, sociologists have for years avoided having to grapple with the evidence or address the arguments. Instead, they attack as 'ideological' any attempt to suggest that intelligence might be linked to social positions, and anyone who takes this possibility seriously is accused of bad faith.[10] Leading French sociologist, Pierre Bourdieu, insists, for example: 'The *ideology of giftedness*, the cornerstone of the whole educational and social system, helps to enclose the under-privileged classes in the role which society has given them by making them see as natural inability things which are only a result of an inferior social status.'[11] Similarly, two of the most influential writers on the American class system reassure us that the 'true function' of IQ testing lies in 'legitimating the social institutions underpinning the stratification system itself'.[12]

Researchers who have insisted on the importance of intelligence have been marginalised, or even banned from speaking or writing. The respected political economist, James Heckman, notes that linking IQ to achievement has 'become "taboo" in respectable academic discourse', and he warns that it is 'folly' for any scholar looking to publish in peer-reviewed journals or to apply for peer-reviewed research funding, to pursue this line of inquiry.[13] This is borne out to some extent by my own experiences,[14] but others have fared much worse. In Britain, Hans Eysenck, a pioneer of research on IQ, was banned by the National Union of Students from speaking on university campuses during the 1970s,[15] and in 1996, *The g factor*, written by an Edinburgh psychologist, Chris Brand, was withdrawn by the publisher on the grounds that it made 'assertions which we find repellent'.[16]

Why IQ must differ by class, but need not differ by race

One reason writers like Eysenck, Jensen and (a generation later) Herrnstein and Murray have attracted such vicious criticism and opposition from academics is that they applied their ideas to racial group differences. This has produced strong emotional reactions,[17] and these have tended to spill over into reactions to research on class and intelligence too.[18] However, there is a crucial difference between the two research topics.

There is no *a priori* reason to believe that average levels of intelligence *should* vary between different racial groups. They might, and they might not—it is for research to determine the question as best it can by means of empirical evidence. But when we turn to consider class, there are good grounds for believing that such differences *should* exist.

Race is what sociologists call an 'ascribed' social role while class is an 'achieved' social role. Our racial identity is normally fixed at birth. Of course there are ambiguities, and racial identities may in this sense be 'socially negotiated', but race is not something which people achieve through their own efforts, and it does not change over one's lifespan as a result of what we achieve. Clever black children do not turn white, and clever white children do not turn Asian.

Class is different. When we are born, we share the class identity of our parents, but this is a temporary identity, pending our own occupational fate once we leave school. Once we become adults, our class depends on what we have achieved, not on how we were born. Class membership is therefore selected and competed for in a way that racial membership is not. And given that one criterion of selection is likely to be intelligence, we should expect to find brighter people moving into the middle class in each generation.

There is no such criterion of selection for race. Clever black children do not change their ethnicity in the way that clever working class children commonly change their class.

Before the 1960s, social scientists (including sociologists) were well aware of the importance of intelligence in influencing educational and occupational success. The 1944 Education Act was introduced precisely to ensure that bright children would be selected for a grammar school education irrespective of their class background, and by the time David Glass conducted his pioneering research in 1949, there was widespread optimism among 'progressives' that this new system would overcome the rigidities associated with the pre-war schooling system.

As time went by, however, it became clear that more middle class than working class children were passing the 11+ examination, and this disturbed the political left.[19] Although large numbers of bright working class children did pass the exam and go on to benefit from a grammar school education, middle class children did even better. There emerged on the left a belief that this was because talented working class children were failing due to disadvantages associated with their social class background.

Through the 1950s and into the 1960s, sociological studies began to report on an apparently huge 'wastage' of working class talent, which was attributed to impoverished or overcrowded housing, lack of parental support for children's school work, institutional bias against children from relatively impoverished backgrounds, and the cultural disadvantages encountered by children using a 'restricted linguistic code' associated with a working class upbringing.[20] The British sociological establishment increasingly came to the view that middle class children were outperforming working class children because the system was unfair. This in turn led to the argument that the 11+ exam was flawed, and that any attempt to select on the basis of intelligence was impossible because intelligence could not accurately be measured, and results were inevitably contaminated by a class bias.

There is little doubt that the 11+ was a blunt instrument for sorting out intellectual sheep and goats, and undoubtedly some bright working class children failed when they 'should' have succeeded, while some dull middle class children passed when they 'should' have failed. The examination tested numeracy and literacy skills, in addition to 'general intelligence' assessed by a verbal reasoning IQ test. Critics claimed with some justification that this tended to favour children from relatively advantaged cultural backgrounds (IQ tests based on non-verbal 'fluid ability' would have been less influenced by cultural background than verbal tests of 'crystallised ability', but these were not always used in the 11+).[21] Selection at 11 also disadvantaged 'late developers', it was deliberately loaded against girls (because girls outperformed boys on average but were subjected to equal gender quotas), and it generated unfair regional biases (because local education authorities differed in the proportions of grammar school places they made available).

Yet despite all this, the system did not misclassify substantial proportions of children. The best evidence for this comes from the work of A.H. Halsey, a colleague of Goldthorpe's on the original social mobility project. Halsey analysed the educational backgrounds and experiences of Goldthorpe's sample of ten thousand men, and his results showed that those born into middle class families were over-represented in selective (state and private) secondary schools.[22] However, he then estimated average IQ scores for individuals from different social class backgrounds on the basis of data collected in the 1950s (when sociologists still believed that such scores meant something and were worth collecting). This produced average IQ estimates of 109 for those originating in the service class, 102 for those from intermediate class backgrounds, and 98 for those born to working class parents. Working with these estimates, Halsey calculated the proportion of children from each class who 'should' have attended a selective school had the system been perfectly meritocratic.

While 72 per cent of service class sons attended selective schools, Halsey's calculations suggested that only 58 per cent were bright enough to have done so. And while 24 per cent of working class sons attended such schools, the calculations indicated that 28 per cent should have done so given their IQ. Halsey saw these results as damning. Referring to the figures for the working class, he wrote: 'A shortfall of four per cent may not sound a very grave departure from meritocracy but in absolute terms it represents a very large number of working class boys... a total of around 6,000 boys from the working class who were denied their meritocratic due *each year*.'[23]

But a shortfall of four percentage points *is* small, especially when we remember that Halsey conflated private and grammar schools in his analysis of 'selective schools' (which inevitably inflated the proportion of middle class children attending them). The key conclusion to take from Halsey's results is that cognitive ability was by far the most important single factor distinguishing those who succeeded under the old 11+ system and those who failed.

What was true of the process of educational selection was also true of the subsequent process of occupational selection. Using the same average IQ estimates that Halsey used, Anthony Heath re-analysed Goldthorpe's social mobility data to take account of differences of intelligence. He found moderately strong associations between people's IQ and their educational success ($r=0.38$), and between their IQ and the eventual social class position they achieved ($r=0.27$). The relationship between their class background and their occupational destination was, however, much weaker. Heath concluded: 'Those circumstances of birth which we can measure do not exert a very powerful constraint on... later achievements.'[24] Put more bullishly, once we look at differences of ability, the strong association which Goldthorpe claimed to have found between class origins and destinations suddenly became an awful lot weaker.

Measuring cognitive ability

Given this sort of evidence, it is clearly crucial that social mobility research should take account of cognitive ability. But for the last forty or fifty years, sociologists have been reluctant to do so. They have denied that intelligence can accurately be measured or assessed by IQ tests; they have rejected the idea that there is any such thing as 'general intelligence' (g), which is what IQ tests claim to measure; and they have dismissed any claim that individual differences in cognitive ability might have any innate or biological foundation. They have instead insisted that IQ tests are culture-bound and class-biased, and that this is why working class children score lower on average than middle class children do.[25]

Most of this scepticism is ill-informed and ill-founded.[26] IQ tests, properly conducted, can and do provide a robust measure of what we think of as 'intelligence'. IQ scores are remarkably stable over long periods of time (one Scottish study re-tested men and women at age 77 and found a correlation of 0.73 with their test scores at age 11).[27] Scores correlate strongly with results of tests of mental skills, such as reading and maths (i.e. they achieve 'external validity'), and scores on different kinds of IQ tests correlate highly with each other (they achieve 'internal validity').

IQ is a good predictor of mental reaction times (e.g. how long it takes you to push a button after a light flashes), inspection times (e.g. how long you need to recognise which of two lines is longer), working memory capacity (how much information you can retain while working on something else), and forward and backward digit span test results (the ability to repeat a sequence of numbers forwards relative to the ability to repeat the same sequence backwards).[28] In addition, IQ scores correlate with directly measured brain activity such as the evoked potentials of brainwaves (Eysenck records correlations as high as 0.6 between IQ scores and speed of brain waves evoked by sudden stimuli of light or sound), positron emission topography (the brains of those with high IQs take up less glucose when solving problems than do the brains of those with low IQs), and the highly heritable condition of myopia.[29] Phenomena like reaction times, brainwave potentials, and positron emissions relate directly to brain processing speed, accuracy and efficiency—factors which are central to intellectual capacity.

The use of an IQ score to summarise somebody's cognitive ability assumes that intelligence is a general characteristic, measurable on a single scale. Although there are different kinds of mental abilities, these are all thought to reflect something called 'general intelligence' (g). For example, people with good spatial ability tend also, on average, to have good verbal ability, good mathematical ability, good logical reasoning ability, and so on. Tests measuring all of these abilities can be shown to reflect a single common factor, so just as we might speak of a general quality of 'athleticism' shared in common by those who are good at sprinting, marathon running and long jumping, so too we can identify a common factor of intelligence underlying a variety of different mental capacities.[30]

Both genetics and environment are almost certainly implicated in intelligence. To the extent that intelligence is genetically determined, it will reflect the interplay of multiple genes, each of which makes a relatively small contribution to the overall variance in mental performance within the population.[31] Similarly, to the extent that it is shaped by environmental factors, many different influences will be involved, including intra- as well as inter-family differences in the way children are nurtured.

Genes and environment interact in quite complex ways. Environmental influences—relations with parents, input from schools, mental exertion and practice, even a mother's diet while the foetus is still in the womb—can change our intellectual capacities and performance. Equally, our genetic inheritance can shape the kinds of environmental influences to which we are exposed. Plomin, for example, suggests that genetic dispositions often lead us into environments which accentuate our genetic propensities (e.g. people with a strong innate ability in some specific mental task often seek out tasks which utilise and therefore develop precisely this capacity). Similarly, factors which we think of as 'environmental' influences on intellectual development may themselves have a genetic component (e.g. parents who enjoy reading will encourage their children to use books, but parents who enjoy reading may do so precisely because they have a high innate verbal ability with a genetic basis which is likely to have been passed on to their children).[32]

Given that intelligence is a function of both 'nature' and 'nurture', and that these two factors are each themselves entailed in the other, it is obviously extremely difficult to partial out their respective influences. But it is not impossible. Hans Eysenck claims that heredity is twice as important as environment in explaining differences in intelligence, and he bases this estimate on the results of repeated experiments carried out over many years by many different researchers.[33] These experiments compare variations in mental ability between people who are unrelated genetically but who share a common environment (e.g. children raised in children's homes) with variations between people who are genetically related but raised in contrasting environments (e.g. twins raised by different sets of foster parents). Many attempts have been made to discredit this work, but his overall conclusion is compelling and incontrovertible.

The strongest experiments focus on the performance of identical (monozygotic) twins as compared with non-identical (dizygotic) twins. MZ twins share all their genes in common while DZ twins share 50 per cent of their genes. Ignoring Cyril Burt's disputed findings, and aggregating the results of other researchers whose integrity has never been questioned, Eysenck reports the following average correlations in intelligence test scores:[34]

- MZ twins raised in the same environment = 0.87

- MZ twins reared in separate environments = 0.77

- DZ twins raised in the same environment = 0.53

These figures compare with an average correlation of 0.23 for biologically unrelated individuals who are raised in a common environment (e.g. adopted or foster children), and with a correlation of zero for unrelated children raised in different environments.

It is clear from these figures that intelligence is not solely genetic (if it were, there would be a perfect correlation of 1.0 between scores of MZ twins, irrespective of whether or not they were raised together, and there would be a zero correlation between scores of unrelated children raised in the same environment). It is also clear, however, that there is a substantial genetic component to intelligence, for variations attributable to separate environments appear much lower than those attributable to different genetic inheritance.

Critics have attempted to dispute this by suggesting that the experimental conditions on which these results depend were often flawed. Kamin, for example, suggests (probably rightly) that twins who are raised separately are often nevertheless brought up in similar environments, and this will tend to underestimate the contribution attributable to environmental factors because the degree of environmental variation is relatively small. He also suggests that studies of adopted and foster children are weakened by the fact that adoption agencies often try to place children in homes similar to those of their natural parents, thus again reducing any potential effect of environmental variation. In the end, however, such criticisms appear trifling, for Kamin cannot refute the strongest evidence from twin studies pointing to a substantial genetic component in measured intelligence. This is the average correlations on IQ test results of 0.77 for MZ twins reared apart as compared with 0.53 for DZ twins reared together.

If environment were more important than heredity, the relative strength of these correlations should be reversed. Identical twins raised separately should differ more in their scores than non-identical twins raised together, for they have been subjected to greater environmental variation. The opposite, however, holds true. Even when brought up separately, identical twins score much more similarly on IQ tests than non-identical twins who were kept together. Kamin accepts that the correlations reported by Eysenck are genuine, and although he quibbles with many of the other findings reported by Eysenck, he can offer no environmental explanation for this, the most crucial of them. To the extent that anything is ever proven in social science, the undisputed fact that identical twins brought up separately correlate so much more highly on test scores than non-identical twins raised together proves that intelligence is based to a substantial degree (perhaps 50 per cent, probably more) on a cluster of genes which we inherit from our parents.

Research on intelligence has clearly demonstrated that we are not all born equal, despite the wishes of egalitarian sociologists that we were. Heckman concludes from his review of the research literature: 'Psychometrics is not a fraud. Tests predict productivity in schools and in the market, and they predict performance in society at large. One linear combination of test scores, g, does remarkably well in synthesizing what a battery of tests predict. Part of the disparity in the performance of demographic groups in schools and the workplace is due to differences in ability.'[35]

This being the case, there is clearly no justification for sociologists to continue ignoring intelligence when they study social mobility.

Modelling class, intelligence and social mobility

Citing American data, Hans Eysenck reports average IQ scores of 128 for accountants and lawyers, 122 for teachers, 109 for electricians, 96 for truck drivers and 91 for miners and farmhands. He also shows correlations as high as 0.81 between IQ scores and incomes, and 0.91 between IQ and occupational prestige (as measured by surveys of how the public ranks different jobs in terms of their social standing). In short, the occupational system does appear (unsurprisingly) to select people by measured cognitive ability.

There is also evidence that men and women tend to end up mating, not only with people from a similar social class, but also with partners with a similar level of IQ to their own. Intelligent women tend, on average, to mate with intelligent men, with the result that they tend to produce intelligent children. Conversely, dull parents tend, on average, to come together to produce dull children.[36]

The cognitive development of children from different class backgrounds

IQ cannot be measured accurately much before the age of ten, but it is possible to give very young children simple tests which are indicative of their cognitive development. These show clear associations between the social class (or income) of parents and the cognitive performance of their children.[37]

Research on the children in the UK Millenium cohort, for example, finds that, at age three, their scores on a 'school readiness' test involving colours, letters, numbers and shapes vary significantly by parental income. Children with parents in the lowest income quintile score an average of 32 per cent on this test, compared with 63 per cent for those whose parents are in the highest quintile. Similarly, the average vocabulary score varies from 35 per cent, for those from the poorest families, to 58 per cent for those with the most affluent parents. This gap in vocabulary scores widens slightly as time goes on, so by age five, average scores are still 35 per cent (for the bottom quintile), but have stretched to 61 per cent (for the top).

Research on the 1970 birth cohort has tracked the cognitive development of children who at 22 months scored in the highest (scores of 90 per cent) and lowest (scores of 10 per cent) quartiles on a simple ability assessment. There was huge variability comparing these scores at 22 months with later scores, which suggests the 22 month tests contained a lot of measurement error, but from 42 months, the scores started to settle down. However, while high-scoring children from higher class backgrounds showed consistency in their cognitive ability scores from the age of 3½ to five and on to age ten, high-scoring children from lower class backgrounds began to tail off. Between the ages of five and ten, their average cognitive performance was overtaken by the higher class children who had originally scored in the bottom quartile when first tested at 22 months. This latter group's performance improved consistently throughout the first ten years of life, suggesting that parents (and possibly schools and neighbourhoods too) were able to raise these children's potential IQ scores through support and stimulus in the early years.

This evidence demonstrates how IQ scores reflect the way parents nurture their children's intellectual capacity, as well as the genes they pass on to them. Class-based transmission of measured intelligence is both environmental and genetic.

Putting these two sets of evidence together, it is clear that working class parents should be expected to produce children whose average IQ will be lower than that of children born to middle class parents. If people entering middle class jobs tend to be more intelligent, and if they select more intelligent partners, then (assuming that intelligence has some genetic basis) it must be the case that the children they produce will tend to be relatively intelligent as well. And this, of course, is precisely what we find. As we saw earlier, research in Britain in the 1950s recorded average IQ scores of 109 for middle class children as compared with 98 for working class children.

The key question then arises: how big a disparity in inter-generational social mobility patterns should we expect to be generated in a purely meritocratic system as a result of class-based IQ differences? Bigger, certainly, than Goldthorpe's criterion of 1:1, but would it be as great as the disparity ratios of 3:1 or 4:1 which he reports from his study of social mobility among males in Britain?

To answer this, we can construct from Goldthorpe's own data a model of what social mobility would look like in a pure meritocracy. Five points need to be emphasised about this exercise:

- First, I am not suggesting that Britain *is* a perfect meritocracy. The point of the exercise is to establish the pattern of social mobility which *would* exist if Britain *were* a perfectly meritocratic society, for this will enable us to compare the reality with the 'perfect' model to gauge the extent to which the reality falls short of the ideal.

- Secondly, the model does not depend on actual IQ test results. To accept the model, it is necessary only to accept that individuals differ in their intellectual abilities, and that the distribution of abilities within each generation is approximately 'normal' (i.e. most people cluster around the average ability level with proportionately fewer at each extreme).[38] We can therefore leave on one side the question of whether actual IQ scores offer a reliable measure of people's cognitive ability, because the model does not use them.

- Thirdly, the model assumes the social class positions of fathers apply equally to mothers (because we are using Goldthorpe's data, we only have information on the fathers). We also assume for the sake of simplicity that parents share the same IQ.

- Fourthly, we ignore the 'intermediate classes' and focus for the sake of simplicity on the rates of interchange which should be expected between working class and 'service class' origins and destinations, for it is here that Goldthorpe reports the most extreme disparity ratios.

- Fifthly, again to keep things simple, we leave aside the second element in the theory of meritocracy, namely 'effort', and concentrate solely on ability (although the way we deduce hypothetical IQ scores could just as well be extended to encompass hypothetical motivation scores as well, provided only that both of these attributes are normally distributed in the population).

The *first step* in constructing the model is to focus on the older of two generations. We know from Goldthorpe's data that, in the fathers' generation, just 14 per cent occupied 'service class' positions while 55 per cent were in working class positions (the remainder were in intermediate positions which we shall ignore). Under conditions of a perfect meritocracy, these fathers would have been recruited to their occupational class positions purely on the basis of their ability (remember that we are ignoring 'effort' for the time being). Thus, had a perfect meritocracy been operating when they were young, we can say that all of the fathers who made it to the service class would have been in the top 14 per cent of the ability distribution in their generation, and that all of the fathers who entered the working class would have been in the bottom 55 per cent of this distribution.

These proportions can be translated into IQ scores. The scale of IQ is normally distributed with a mean (average) score of 100 and a standard deviation of 15 (the 'standard deviation' expresses the average amount

61

by which any one person selected at random is likely to differ from the mean score). From this, we can calculate that the top 14 per cent of the ability distribution should all score 116 or higher on IQ tests, while the bottom 55 per cent should all score 102 or less. Thus, had Britain been a perfect meritocracy, all of the service class fathers would have had an IQ of 116 or better, and all the working class fathers would have had an IQ no higher than 102.

The *second step* in the model is to develop the same calculations for the sons' generation. Goldthorpe's data tell us that, in the sons' generation, 27 per cent were in service class jobs while 44 per cent were in the working class. The substantial difference between the size of these classes in each of the two generations is explained by the expansion of middle class employment and the contraction in working class employment during the intervening period (the increasing 'room at the top' of the occupational class system). It follows that, had the sons been recruited to their jobs purely on meritocratic criteria, the top 27 per cent of the ability distribution would have ended up in the service class and the bottom 44 per cent would have gravitated to the working class. Sons entering the service class should all therefore have had an IQ of 109 or higher, while those entering the working class would have had an IQ at or below 98.

In the *third step* in the model, we have to calculate the statistical probabilities of sons ending up in the same social class as their fathers if occupational placement in both generations took place purely on the basis of intelligence. How likely is it, for example, that middle class fathers with an IQ of 116 or more would produce sons with an IQ of 109 or more (the minimum score necessary if they are to follow in their fathers' footsteps)?

To answer this, we have to estimate the correlation between fathers' IQ scores and those of their sons. It is sometimes thought that class positions in a truly meritocratic society would increasingly be inherited since bright parents in the top classes will produce bright children who will themselves then enter the top classes, and so on down the generations.[39] But this would only be the case if there were close to a perfect correlation between the IQ of parents and that of their children. In reality, while bright parents tend to produce bright children, not all their children will be bright (the correlation is above 0 but less than 1). The result is that, on average, the IQ of their children will actually be lower than that of the parents as it regresses towards the mean IQ score for the whole population.[40] In a perfect meritocracy, downward mobility will be the result. (The reverse, of course, is true for children born to dull parents, who will tend to have IQs higher than those of their parents, and who in meritocratic conditions will therefore tend to move up the class system).[41]

In our model of expected social mobility patterns in a perfect meritocracy, we impute a correlation of 0.5 between parents' and children's IQ scores. This is the correlation implied by data on the association between social class and IQ cited by Eysenck.[42] It is also the average correlation between the IQ scores of children and their natural parents reported in 212 different studies across the world.[43] If it is wrong, then the model will not fit Goldthorpe's data when we come to apply it.

The *fourth step* in constructing our model is to calculate the proportion of children from each social class who would end up in various different class locations under conditions of perfect meritocracy. Four patterns have to be established:

- *Middle class children eligible for middle class entry:* We calculated earlier that, had they been recruited purely on the basis of intelligence, the middle class fathers in Goldthorpe's survey should all have had an IQ of 116 or above. We also saw that the expansion of the middle class has meant that, for the sons of these fathers, the IQ threshold for middle class entry would have fallen to 109. Assuming a correlation of 0.5 between parents' and children's IQ scores, we can calculate that 59 per cent of children produced by parents with an IQ of 116 or more would have an IQ of 109 or above. A model of social mobility under conditions of perfect meritocracy would therefore predict that 59 per cent of the children born into the middle class will be bright enough to stay there.

- *Middle class children eligible only for working class entry:* In the sons' generation, we calculated earlier that only those with an IQ of 98 or less would enter the working class, assuming purely meritocratic recruitment. What is the probability of parents with an IQ of 116 or more producing children with an IQ of 98 or less? Assuming a correlation on IQ scores of 0.5, the answer is that 21 per cent of the children of these parents would score this low. Our model of perfect meritocracy therefore predicts that 21 per cent of the sons of middle class fathers would end up in working class jobs.

- *Working class children eligible for middle class entry:* We saw earlier that working class fathers would all have had an IQ of 102 or less if they had been recruited to their class positions purely on the basis of ability. Given an IQ threshold of 109 for entry into the middle class in the sons' generation, we can calculate that 18 per cent of the sons of these fathers would have an IQ high enough to qualify.

- *Working class children eligible only for working class entry:* The upper IQ limit for entry into the working class in the sons' generation is 98. Of those born to parents with an IQ no higher than 102, 58 per cent would be predicted to have an IQ of 98 or less. Our model therefore predicts that, under conditions of perfect meritocracy, 58 per cent of the children born to working class parents will remain in the working class.

Having calculated all the predicted class destinations of children born to middle class and working class parents, the model can now be compared with the actual pattern of social mobility between these two classes recorded by Goldthorpe's 1972 survey (Table 7).

Table 7

A comparison of actual rates of social mobility with the rates predicted by a model of perfect meritocracy[44]

Mobility Pattern	Predicted %	Actual %
Service class > service class	59	59
Service class > working class	21	15
Working class > service class	18	16
Working class > working class	58	57

This table reveals an extraordinarily high degree of fit between Goldthorpe's findings and a model of perfect meritocracy. With the sole exception of downward mobility from the middle class into the working class (where the actual rate of movement is about 25 per cent less than that predicted), the model fits Goldthorpe's data almost exactly. *The social mobility histories of the ten thousand men interviewed for Goldthorpe's study in 1972 are almost precisely what we would have expected to find had they and their fathers been recruited to their class positions purely on the basis of their intelligence.*

The implications of this finding can hardly be exaggerated. Rarely in social science are we able to develop simple models which fit the empirical evidence so closely. What Table 7 tells us is that, assuming only that intelligence is normally distributed in the population, and that there is a correlation of 0.5 between the intelligence of parents and that of their children, then patterns of social mobility found by Goldthorpe in 1972 correspond almost exactly with the patterns which would be found if class recruitment were based solely on differences of intelligence between individuals.

Goldthorpe, remember, asserted that a disparity ratio as high as 4:1 could not possibly be the product of differences in average levels of intelligence between the classes. He dismissed the idea as 'social Darwinist' and 'Smilesian'. Yet we now see that this is precisely the sort of ratio which we should expect to find if class recruitment were based solely on intelligence. Once we allow for the differences in average levels of intelligence which would exist between classes recruited on meritocratic principles, we find that what Goldthorpe described as the 'gross' advantages enjoyed by middle class children in Britain all but disappear. Goldthorpe's 4:1 disparity ratio in favour of those born into the middle class compares with an advantage when allowance is made for transmission of intelligence across the generations of just 1.4:1 in favour of the middle class child avoiding a working class destination, and no advantage at all when considering the relative chances of children from different backgrounds entering the middle class. Once we take account of ability differences, in other words, we end up at or very close to Goldthorpe's own criterion of social fairness, a disparity ratio of 1:1.

This does not mean the meritocracy thesis has been proven, only that it remains plausible in the light of Goldthorpe's data. The fact that our model of a perfect meritocracy is remarkably consistent with the data on social mobility does not mean that the model is necessarily the 'correct' one for interpreting these data. We have demonstrated that the patterns reported by Goldthorpe are almost certainly being produced by some factor or cluster of factors which is normally distributed and correlated at around 0.5 as between parents and their children. Intelligence fits the bill, but so too might other things which we have not considered in this chapter (including, of course, motivation, the other pillar of the meritocracy thesis).

All that can be concluded at this stage, therefore, is that intelligence cannot be ruled out. But this is a substantial conclusion to reach given the history of research on social mobility in Britain. It means that the meritocracy thesis is wholly consistent with the evidence on social mobility, despite the claims of sundry professors down the years that it is not. It also means that British sociologists are obliged to address the possibility that we do, after all, live in a broadly meritocratic society.

5

Is Britain a Meritocracy?

At ages 7, 11 and 16, the children in the NCDS survey all sat maths and English tests, and at 11 they also took a (non-standardised) general ability test consisting of eighty verbal and non-verbal items. The scores all correlate highly, and analysis of scores on the general ability test reveals two important findings (Table 8).[1]

Table 8
Mean ability scores by class of origin (higher parental class)
and class of destination

Class of origin	Mean	Standard Deviation	Class of destination	Mean	Standard Deviation
I/II	50.6	14.3	I/II	51.6	13.7
III	44.0	15.0	III	42.2	14.7
IV/V	40.2	15.3	IV/V	36.3	14.8

r=0.24 (N=5565, missing=1230) r=0.37 (N=5826, missing=969)

(Mean test score for total sample = 45.4 on 80 items, standard deviation = 14.3)

First, the children's scores reflected to some extent the social class of their parents (social class is defined here according to the OPCS 5-class schema).[2] We can see that there was a clear and consistent gradient in mean (average) test scores between those with fathers or mothers in class I/II and those whose parents were in classes IV and V. We also see that parental class and children's test scores correlate with a coefficient (r) of 0.24. This indicates that the parents' class and the children's test scores are related, though not particularly strongly.

Both the SAD and the meritocracy hypotheses would expect to discover a correlation like this. For the former, it is the result of social advantages which enable middle class children to 'over-achieve' on ability tests. For the latter, it is evidence that bright middle class parents tend to produce and raise bright children while less bright working class parents tend to produce and raise children of lower average ability.

The second key finding is that test scores correlate much more strongly (r=0.37) with the social class achieved by the children twenty-two years after taking the test, than with the class of their parents around the time that they sat it. Again, there is a clear gradient in scores ranging from those entering class I/II to those entering class IV/V, but the higher correlation is due mainly to a much more marked association between ability and class of destination at the lower end of the class hierarchy. Individuals ending up in classes IV and V have markedly lower IQ scores.

This result is consistent with the meritocracy thesis, but not with the SAD thesis. In a meritocratic class system we would expect bright parents often to produce bright children, but we know that some bright parents will produce dull children, just as some dull parents will produce bright ones. Because a meritocratic class system will select able children for higher positions regardless of their social background, the association between class of origin and ability should be weaker than that between ability and class of destination, and this is indeed what we find. The particularly strong association between low ability and low class destinations indicates that bright children are tending to avoid class IV/V entry and are to some extent being selected for higher positions. This is contrary to the SAD hypothesis which would predict associations of equal strength since ability is seen merely as a correlate of class background and should not itself contribute to the determination of class of destination.

It is clear that ability does play some part in influencing class destinations. But could social class differences in ability alone account for the disparity ratios found in mobility tables in both the Goldthorpe and the NCDS data?

By age 33, 43 per cent of the NCDS sample were in class I/II occupations. The score achieved on the ability test by the top 43 per cent of children was 49 or above (out of a total of 80). If class positions achieved by age 33 simply reflected ability as measured at age 11, then we would expect all those achieving class I/II positions to have scored 49 or better on the ability test. We find, however, that only 62 per cent of those entering class I/II scored this highly. Put crudely, 38 per cent of those arriving in class I/II were not bright enough to be there. Here we have the first indication that class destinations reflect more than just ability.

Focusing on the less able entrants to class I/II (those scoring less than 49), we find that twice as many (32 per cent) came from class I/II backgrounds as from class IV/V backgrounds (17 per cent). Looking at the data in a different way, and focusing on the lowest quartile of ability across the whole sample, we find that 41 per cent of low ability children from class I/II origins still managed to gain entry to class I/II as compared with 21 per cent of low ability children from class IV/V origins. Low ability middle class children are therefore twice as likely to succeed as low ability children from semi- and unskilled manual worker homes, although even among the latter, around one-fifth still arrive in the middle class despite low ability scores at age 11. It is clear from this that low ability is not necessarily a barrier to later occupational success. Conversely, high ability does appear to offer a reasonable guarantee against failure, for only five per cent of children in the top ability quartile ended up in class IV/V while 65 per cent of them made it to class I/II.[3]

Table 9
Social Mobility Disparity Ratios above and below threshold ability score for class I/II entry (whole sample in brackets)

(a) Those scoring high enough for class I/II entry:

	Relative chances of being in:	
	Class I/II	Class IV/V
Father class I/II	1.67 (2.21)	set at 1
Father class III	1.23 (1.29)	1.71 (2.18)
Father class IV/V	set at 1	3.50 (3.47)

(b) Those scoring below threshold entry for class I/II:

	Relative chances of being in:	
	Class I/II	Class IV/V
Father class I/II	2.13 (2.21)	set at 1
Father class III	1.15 (1.29)	1.72 (2.18)
Father class IV/V	set at 1	2.31 (3.47)

Ability, then, is part of the explanation for why middle class children are more successful than working class children, but it is not the full story. We can gauge how important it is by calculating a modified set of disparity ratios dividing the sample into those with an ability score high enough to warrant entry to class I/II and those scoring below this threshold point (Table 9). The first part of Table 9 shows (first cell) that the relative advantage enjoyed by class I/II children over class IV/V children in achieving a middle class destination is reduced to just 1.7:1 once we control for ability. The second part of Table 9 shows (last cell) that middle class children reduce their relative chances of avoiding class IV/V from 3.5:1 to 2.3:1 once we control for ability. Summarising all this, it seems that differences in average ability levels between children of different classes explain about half of the disparity in their relative chances of achieving middle class entry and avoiding lower working class entry.

Testing the meritocracy thesis against the SAD thesis

Ability is only one part of the meritocracy thesis. The other key element is 'effort' which involves both the desire to succeed and a commitment to behaviour (e.g. hard work) which is likely to bring success. In a meritocratic society, bright individuals will only succeed if they are motivated to do so, and people of lesser ability may still achieve relatively high positions if they are committed, motivated and hard-working. A rigorous test of the meritocracy thesis thus requires adequate measures of effort as well as ability.

In the NCDS survey, there are various possible indicators of 'effort'. We shall examine (a) a motivation scale based on attitude questions answered by the children at age 16 (MOTIVATION)[4]; (b) an 'absent-eeism' factor based on school truancy records and reports of trivial absences (ABSENTEEISM); and (c) a 'job commitment' factor based on answers to three attitude questions at age 33 (WORK ATTITUDES). Taken together with the ability scores at age 11 (ABILITY TEST SCORE), these represent the major indicators for testing the meritocracy thesis.

To compare the meritocratic explanation of social mobility rates with the 'SAD' explanation (the view that mobility chances reflect the 'social advantages and disadvantages' associated with people's class origins), we need also to identify a series of indicators for evaluating the SAD thesis. One, clearly, is parental class (PARENTAL CLASS) which is measured according to the social class of father or mother when the child was aged 16, whichever is the higher. Linked to this is the educational level of the parents, for this will affect what Bourdieu calls the 'cultural capital' that can be passed on to children, and it may also influence the values which parents have and the decisions they make regarding the importance of a good education for their children. For fathers (FATHERS EDUCATION) and mothers (MOTHERS EDUCATION), education is measured as a dichotomous variable based on whether or not they completed their schooling at the minimum leaving age. Other variables and factors measuring possible class advantages/disadvantages associated with social background include the higher class of either grandfather (GRANDPARENTS CLASS), a measure of overcrowding in the home based on persons per room while the children were growing up (OVERCROWDING), and a measure of lack of basic amenities in the home (HOME AMENITIES).

Also related to the SAD thesis are a number of variables and factors associated with the education of the child and the support it received from the parents. PRE-SCHOOL EDUCATION indicates whether or not children attended any pre-school or nursery education facility before the age of five, and TYPE OF SCHOOL distinguishes those receiving a private education at 16 from those attending state schools. FATHER READ and MOTHER READ indicate the degree to which father and mother respectively read to the child at age seven, and PARENTAL INTEREST is a measure of parental interest in the schooling of the child at age 11 based upon the school's assessment of the interest demonstrated by the father and mother plus evidence on whether they had made contact with the school during the previous twelve months. PARENTAL ASPIRATIONS expresses the degree to which parents had high aspirations for their child at age 11 (based on their wish that the child should remain at school beyond the minimum leaving age, and their hope that it should go on to some form of further education). Finally, the sex of the child is measured by GENDER.

Taken together, these thirteen measures cover many of the material and cultural advantages/disadvantages which sociologists down the years have identified in an attempt to explain why class origins should be expected to influence educational and occupational success later in life. Not everything has been included—there are no measures of peer group pressure, the quality of interaction with teachers, or the strength of social networks. Nevertheless, the range of measures that are included offers a fair basis for testing most of the fundamental claims on which the SAD thesis rests.

Table 10
A Logistic Regression model predicting the probability that class IV/V children will enter class I/II against the probability of their remaining in class IV/V

STEP	VARIABLE	% OF CASES CORRECTLY PREDICTED	FINAL R (partial correlation coefficient)	FINAL EXP (B) (change in odds for each unit increase)
0		58.5		
1	ABILITY TEST SCORE	69.6	0.26	1.06
2	MOTIVATION	73.0	0.16	0.90
3	WORK ATTITUDES	74.1	0.15	1.59
4	GENDER (FEMALE)	75.7	0.10	2.05
5	GRANDPARENTS CLASS	76.0	0.09	0.63

Variables not in the equation: MOTHER READ, FATHER READ, MOTHER EDUCATION, FATHER EDUCATION, PRESCHOOL EDUCATION, TYPE OF SCHOOL, HOME AMENITIES, OVERCROWDING, PARENTAL ASPIRATIONS, PARENTAL INTEREST, ABSENTEEISM
N=441

We can begin our empirical evaluation of the meritocracy and SAD theses by considering why some working class children succeed when others do not, and why some middle class children fail when others maintain or enhance the position achieved by their parents.

Table 10 gives the results of a 'logistic regression model' in which 4 meritocracy variables and 12 SAD variables are used to predict whether individuals born to class IV/V parents will remain where they are or move all the way up to class I/II (we ignore the 'intermediate classes', IIIN and IIIM). It demonstrates clearly that it is the meritocratic variables—ability, motivation and attitudes to employment—which are the key factors distinguishing successful lower working class children from those they leave behind them.

With 183 of these individuals ending up in class IV/V as compared with 258 ending up in class I/II, the best initial prediction that we can make of any class IV/V individual's class destination is that he or she makes it to class I/II. Such a prediction will be accurate in 59 per cent of cases (the first line in the '% CORRECT' column of the table). We now try to improve this predictive accuracy by taking account of additional information. The model tells us that the single most important piece of information which we need to take into account is the ability test score achieved by these individuals when they were 11 years old. When these test scores are entered into our model (step 1), the accuracy of the predictions rises sharply from 59 per cent correct to 70 per cent correct. We can improve this still further (step 2) by taking account of the level of motivation at school when aged 16 (this information improves our predictive accuracy by a further three per cent). One of the two remaining meritocracy indicators (work attitudes in adult life), plus two of the SAD indicators (gender—women do better than men; and grandfathers' class—those with grandfathers above class IV/V perform better) also have effects significant enough for them to be included in the final model, but together they only raise the level of predictive accuracy by a further three percentage points.

In addition to telling us how powerfully we can predict the class destination of people born to lower working class parents, the model in Table 10 also tells us the relative contribution made by each factor in influencing this outcome. This is expressed by the 'partial correlation coefficients' (FINAL R) which indicate the relative effect of each variable in the model when the effects of all other variables are taken into account. It is clear that ability (R=0.26) is by far the strongest influence, with motivation (R=0.16) and attitudes to work (R=0.15) as contributory factors.

The final column in the table (FINAL EXP B) tells us how much the odds of entering class I/II change for each unit increase in the variable in question. For example, the odds of a class IV/V child entering class I/II relative to the odds of remaining in class IV/V are 258/183=1:1.4. These odds are improved by (1.4x1.06) for each point scored on the ability test, by (1.4x0.9) for each point on the motivation scale,[5] by (1.4x2.05) if the individual is female, and so on.

One of the most striking features of Table 10 concerns the list of variables which fail to enter the model. Some, like private schooling, are hardly surprising, for very few of these children attended fee-paying schools. Others, however, are surprising from the perspective of the SAD hypothesis. Material deprivation in the home (measured by overcrowding and by lack of basic amenities) has no significant effect. Nor do parental levels of education, exposure to books at an early age, pre-school play group or nursery attendance, parental interest in the child's schooling, or parental aspirations for the child's future. To the extent that we can predict success for children from classes IV and V, the key factors have to do with their ability and their attitudes to work (at school and in later employment) and have very little or nothing to do with material conditions or 'cultural capital' in the home.

It is worth emphasising that the possibility of a 'class bias' in the IQ test that these children took can be discounted as an explanation for these findings, for all the children we are considering here came from similar class backgrounds. Clearly, the test results point to real differences in cognitive aptitudes which cannot be explained away as the result of a privileged background.

Now look at Table 11 which outlines a similar logistic regression model, this time predicting failure (downward mobility out of class I/II) of middle class children. Again, the basic message is the same—ability is the key factor with an R (0.19) twice as strong as that of any other variable in the model, and motivation is entered second. Private schooling appears as the most important of the SAD indicators, suggesting that private schools may offer middle class parents some means of insuring their less able offspring against downward mobility. Parental education levels, absenteeism at school, attitudes to work and gender (where this time males prove rather more successful than females) all achieve statistical significance but make only tiny contributions to the final model (indeed, adding gender to the model slightly decreases its explanatory power).

Clearly, for children from similar backgrounds, success or failure depends much more on IQ and motivation than on, say, the aspirations of parents or the type of school attended. The key question, however, is whether ability and effort still outweigh social advantages and disadvantages when we compare children growing up in *different* social classes.

One way of answering this is to compare the ability test scores of downwardly mobile middle class children and upwardly mobile working class children. Class I/II children who retained their middle class position achieved an average score of 54.2 on the general ability test they sat at age 11. Those who fell to class III, however, scored an average of only 46.2, and those who fell to class IV/V managed just 41.5. Meanwhile, class IV/V children who achieved entry to class I/II had an average score of 47.2 as compared with 39.0 for those entering class III and just 33.0 for those who stayed in class IV/V.

Table 11

A Logistic Regression model predicting class I/II children entering class I/II against those who are downwardly mobile

STEP	VARIABLE	% CORRECT	FINAL R	FINAL EXP (B)
0		60.0		
1	ABILITY TEST SCORE	66.1	0.19	1.04
2	MOTIVATION	66.6	0.10	0.94
3	TYPE OF SCHOOL	67.5	0.07	1.92
4	MOTHERS EDUCATION	67.7	0.05	1.36
5	ABSENTEEISM	68.1	0.04	0.79
6	FATHERS EDUCATION	68.1	0.04	1.34
7	WORK ATTITUDES	68.9	0.04	1.15
8	GENDER (MALE)	68.7	0.04	0.76

Variables not in the equation: MOTHER READ, FATHER READ, PRESCHOOL EDUCATION, GRANDPARENTS CLASS, HOME AMENITIES, OVER-CROWDING, PARENTAL ASPIRATIONS, PARENTAL INTEREST

N=1830

These are statistically highly significant differences.[6] Not only do ability scores within each class of origin sharply distinguish those who later succeed from those who do not, but *class IV/V children entering the middle class have significantly higher average ability scores than class I/II children leaving it.* Given that the IQ test sat by these children may to some extent have favoured those from middle class homes (the 'cultural bias' problem we discussed in the last chapter), this is a particularly striking result. Despite the cultural advantages which might have been expected to inflate their test scores, the middle class failures scored lower on average than the successful children from the least advantaged semi-skilled and unskilled manual worker backgrounds. Clearly, the occupational system has sorted these individuals by intelligence to a much greater extent than it has selected them according to their class origins.

We can further evaluate the relative importance of ability and effort on the one hand, and social advantages and disadvantages on the other, by developing a least squares 'multiple regression model'[7] which includes all the meritocracy and SAD indicators and which sorts them out in terms of the relative contribution they make to people's final class destinations. To do this, we have to abandon our social class categories in a favour of a continuous scale which measures people's destinations at age 33 in terms of the prestige of their jobs.[8] All of the variables entered into the model are the same as in Tables 10 and 11, and the results are summarised in Table 12.

Table 12
A Multiple Regression model with occupational prestige score
at age 33 as dependent variable[9]

STEP	VARIABLE	CHANGE IN R^2	FINAL BETA
1	ABILITY TEST SCORE	0.14	0.25
2	MOTIVATION	0.16	0.13
3	PARENTAL CLASS	0.18	0.08
4	ABSENTEEISM	0.19	0.07
5	MOTHERS EDUCATION	0.20	0.06
6	WORK ATTITUDES	0.20	0.07
7	GENDER (MALE)	0.21	0.07
8	FATHERS EDUCATION	0.21	0.05
9	PARENTAL INTEREST	0.22	0.05
10	TYPE OF SCHOOL	0.22	0.05
11	OVERCROWDING	0.22	0.03

Variables not in the equation: FATHER READ, MOTHER READ, PRESCHOOL EDUCATION, GRANDPARENTS CLASS, HOME AMENITIES

In Table 12, the 'CHANGE IN R2' column tells us how well the model is predicting occupational status at each step in its construction. For example, at step 1, we include ability test scores as the single most powerful predictor of people's occupational status at age 33, and these scores immediately explain 14 per cent of the variance in occupational statuses. At step 2, the next most powerful predictor, motivation, is added, and this raises the proportion of variance explained by the model to 16 per cent. And so on. The standardised Beta coefficients in the last column of the table express the relative strength of each item in the model, after allowing for associations between the items. For example, with a coefficient of 0.25, the ability test scores have an effect on occupational status which is twice as strong as motivation (0.13), three times as strong as class background (0.8), and so on.

All four of the meritocracy variables enter the model, but as before, ability is entered first and has by far the strongest effect (Beta=0.25) of any of the variables in the model, while motivation at school enters second (Beta=0.13) and absenteeism at school and work attitudes enter fourth and sixth respectively, each with Betas=0.07. The strongest SAD variable in the model is parental class (Beta=0.08). Parental education levels, gender, parental interest in the child's schooling, private schooling and overcrowding in the home all achieve statistically significant effects, but they make only a tiny contribution to the overall model fit. Grandparents' social class, pre-school education, early exposure to books and the level of basic amenities in the home all fail to achieve statistical significance. The model improves hardly at all after step 4, so to the extent that we can predict someone's occupational status at age 33, it depends mainly on their ability, motivation, parental class and absenteeism. Of these four, ability appears roughly twice as important as motivation and three times more important than parental class and absenteeism.

The final model R-square (the total proportion of variance explained by the model) of 0.22 is, however, fairly weak. The meritocracy thesis appears much stronger than the SAD thesis, but even when the two are combined, over three-quarters of the variance in occupational prestige scores remains unexplained. In part, this is because the model does not include direct measures of achievement which are obvious stepping stones to later occupational success.

Three important measures are examination success at school, the occupational status of the first job taken after completing full-time education, and the achievement of further qualifications after leaving school. These three variables have been excluded until now because they are common to both the meritocracy and SAD theses (both accept that formal qualifications are important in influencing inter-generational mobility chances, and both accept that initial entry into the labour market is an important pointer to final class of destination). But if we add them to our analysis (Table 13), the final model fit is improved substantially (R-square=0.32).

All three new variables are entered into the model before any of the meritocracy or SAD variables. With Beta values of 0.19 and 0.22 respectively, the model clearly demonstrates the influence on final occupational status of formal qualifications achieved at school and subsequently. The status of first job plays an important but less powerful role in the model (the NCDS panel members have undergone substantial intra-generational as well as intergenerational mobility).

The only other variable which continues to have a relatively strong, independent, effect on class of destination is ability (Beta=0.13). This suggests that bright people tend to end up in higher status jobs, partly because they accumulate more qualifications, but also because their ability comes to be recognised and rewarded independently of their paper qualifications.

Table 13
A Multiple Regression model including qualifications
and status of first job as independent variables

STEP	VARIABLE	CHANGE IN R^2	FINAL BETA
1	EXAM PASSES AT 16	0.23	0.19
2	FURTHER QUALS	0.28	0.22
3	CLASS FIRST JOB	0.30	0.13
4	ABILITY TEST SCORE	0.31	0.13
5	PARENTAL CLASS	0.31	0.06
6	ABSENTEEISM	0.32	0.04
7	GENDER (MALE)	0.32	0.05
8	MOTIVATION	0.32	0.05
9	WORK ATTITUDES	0.32	0.04
10	OVERCROWDING	0.32	0.03

Variables not in the equation: MOTHERS EDUCATION, FATHERS EDUCATION, MOTHER READ, FATHER READ, PRESCHOOL EDUCATION, TYPE OF SCHOOL, GRANDPARENTS CLASS, HOME AMENITIES, PARENTAL INTEREST

Looking at Tables 12 and 13, it is striking how many of the factors which have attracted so much academic attention from sociologists down the years—private schooling, parental contact with schools, material conditions in the home, the 'cultural capital' passed on by middle class parents to their children, and even gender bias in the school or the workplace—turn out, even when statistically significant, to exert only relatively minor effects on people's class destinations. By contrast, the factors which sociologists have so often ignored or dismissed—factors having to do with the intellectual capacities of individuals and the tenacity they display in working towards a given objective—turn out to be much more important. The high degree of variance left unexplained by these models suggests there are other factors at work which have little to do with either social advantage/ disadvantage or meritocracy. Nevertheless, they do conclusively demonstrate that the occupational class system in Britain is more meritocratic than has commonly been assumed, and that class origins are much less significant than has generally been claimed. In a straight evaluation of the meritocratic and SAD theses as explanations of social mobility and class recruitment, the former receives much more empirical support than the latter.

Paths to success

Figure 1 (p. 86) sets out what is called a 'path model', based on a set of linear structural equations. This model enables us to unpack the way variables are interconnected and to distinguish their direct and indirect effects on occupational achievement.[10] As before, it aims to predict people's occupational prestige at age 33, but it concentrates only on the 4,298 men in the NCDS survey who were in full-time employment at that time and for whom there is adequate information (the equivalent path model for women is very similar).

The model was constructed using 70 different measures taken from the NCDS at its various 'sweeps' between 1958 and 1991. These are organised sequentially, so looking from left to right of Figure 1, we move from indicators measured in 1958, when the children were born, through indicators measured at ages 7, 11 and 16, to those measured in 1991, when the panel members were aged 33. Indicators in boxes are *variables* which were directly measured in the survey (father's education, for example, is based on a question which asked the age at which panel members' fathers completed their full-time education). Indicators in circles are derived *factors* based on a weighted combination of variables from the survey which are closely associated with one another (academic ability at age 7, for example, is derived from the scores on both the English and Maths tests which children took in 1965, while academic ability at 11 is based on the English and Maths scores in 1969 as well as the results of the general ability test taken at that time).

The straight line arrows running between the different variables and factors in the diagram indicate a causal influence (curved double-headed arrows indicate correlation without imputed causation), and the coefficients on each arrow are the standardised (Beta) weights (similar to the Beta coefficients in the multiple regression models outlined in Tables 12 and 13) which tell us the relative strength of the different

79

causal connections. For example, there are four straight line arrows running from academic ability at age 7. The strongest (r=0.71) runs to academic ability at age 11 (this tells us that scores on the English and Maths tests taken at age 7 are very strongly predictive of scores on the English, Maths and general ability tests taken four years later). Other effects are somewhat weaker but are still quite powerful: the child's ability at 7 influences the child's aspirations at 11 (r=0.30), the parents' aspirations for the child at age 11 (r=0.27), and the parents' lack of interest in the child's education at 11 (the negative coefficient of -0.24 indicating that high ability scores produce low levels of 'lack of interest' —in other words, high interest).

The model outlined in Figure 1 is the simplest we could achieve (i.e. the smallest number of variables, and the smallest number of arrows) while still achieving an acceptable level of fit with the data.[11] Variables which had virtually no influence on other variables in the model were removed (this was true, for example, of pre-school education, and of parents who read to their children at 7 as compared with those who did not). Similarly, absence of an arrow between any two variables or factors indicates there is no significant direct effect linking one to the other, or that the effect is so weak that it can be excluded without seriously weakening overall model fit. Attendance at private school at the age of 7, for example, reduces parental lack of interest in the child's education at age 11 (r=-0.08), but there is no arrow to the child's aspirations at age 11, because private schooling at 7 had little or no impact on children's aspirations four years later.

The fact that there is no direct effect (i.e. no arrow) between two variables or factors does not necessarily mean that the first is having no significant influence on the second, for its effect may be indirect via some third variable or factor in the model. Private schooling at 7, for example, has no *direct* effect on the child's aspirations at 11, but we can trace an *indirect* effect via parental lack of interest in the child's education (because arrows link private schooling to parental interest, and parental interest to the child's aspirations). This suggests that private schooling at 7 increases the level of parental interest at 11 which in turn raises the child's aspirations. To calculate the strength of indirect effects like this, we multiply the coefficients along the arrows which link them (in this example, -0.08 x -0.19, which gives an effect of private schooling on children's aspirations of 0.015). By tracing the different pathways through the model, it is therefore possible to calculate for any given variable both the direct effects and the indirect effects which it has on the final outcome (occupational prestige at age 33), and if we sum the direct and indirect effects, we can find the total effect of each variable or factor. This has been done in Table 14.[12]

Before considering Table 14, it is worth inspecting the path diagram visually. There are only four arrows pointing to occupational prestige at age 33. The two strongest come from qualifications achieved after leaving school ($r=0.25$) and from ability measured at age 11 ($r=0.25$). These direct effects are twice as strong as academic qualifications achieved at school ($r=0.13$) and motivation at school at age 16 ($r=0.13$). There is no direct effect from any of the social background variables. This confirms our earlier results: the strong direct influences on class destination are those which have to do with the individual's ability, motivation and qualifications.

As we move backwards through the diagram, however, we find that other factors are having some indirect effect. To some extent, this further strengthens the initial conclusion that ability is a crucial influence, for not only does ability at 11 directly affect class at 33 ($r=0.25$), but it also has numerous indirect effects which have to be added in too. For example, the path from ability at 11, via qualifications at 16, to class at 33 shows an additional (indirect) effect of ability at 11 of ($0.34 \times 0.13 = 0.044$); the path from ability at 16, via qualifications at 16, to class at 33 shows an additional indirect effect of ($0.11 \times 0.13 = 0.014$); and so on. But taking account of indirect effects also reveals the way social background influences class destination. Father's class has no direct effect, for example, but there are many indirect effects (e.g. father's class when the child was 11 influences the child's motivation at 16 [$r=0.21$] which in turn influences class at 33 [$r=-0.13$] — an indirect effect of 0.028).

Once we begin tracing long and complex paths of indirect causation, the diagram becomes almost unintelligible, and at this point we need to turn to the summary statistics in Table 14. This table gives the stand-ardised direct effect of each variable or factor on the occupational status these men achieved at 33, together with the summed indirect effects along all the possible pathways. The final column calculates the total effect, the sum of these two. This final column confirms that, taking account of all the indirect as well as direct effects, individual

81

characteristics far outweigh the impact of social background and parental influence.

Table 14
Summary of Standardised Direct, Indirect and Total Effects

	DIRECT EFFECT	INDIRECT EFFECTS	TOTAL EFFECTS
(A) SOCIAL ADVANTAGES/DISADVANTAGES			
a.1: Parents class and education:			
Grandparents class	-	0.05	0.05
Mother's education level	-	0.09	0.09
Father's education level	-	0.09	0.09
Father's class in 1958	-	0.12	0.12
Father's class in 1965 (additional effect)	-	0.18	0.18
Father's class in 1969 (additional effect)	-	0.03	0.03
Father's class in 1974 (additional effect)	-	0.03	0.03
Mother's class in 1974	-	0.01	0.01
a.2: Housing conditions			
Crowded accommodation at age 7	-	0.03	0.03
Crowded at age 11 (additional effect)		0.02	0.02
Crowded at age 16 (additional effect)		0.01	0.01
a.3: Schooling			
Private school at age 7		0.01	0.01
Private school age 16 (additional effect)		0.02	0.02
(B) PARENTS BEHAVIOUR/ATTITUDES			
b.1: Aspirations for child			
When child aged 7	-	-	-
When aged 11 (additional effect)	-	0.04	0.04
When aged 16 (additional effect)	-	0.13	0.13
b.2: Interest in child's education			
When child aged 7		0.14	0.14
When aged 11 (additional effect)		0.09	0.09
When aged 16 (additional effect)		0.07	0.07

Table cont'd over

	DIRECT EFFECT	INDIRECT EFFECTS	TOTAL EFFECTS
(C) INDIVIDUAL CHARACTERISTICS			
c.1: Academic ability			
Aged 7	-	0.39	0.39
Aged 11 (additional effect)	0.25	0.18	0.43
Aged 16 (additional effect)	-	0.03	0.03
c.2: Ambition			
Child's aspirations aged 11	-	0.15	0.15
Child's aspirations aged 16 (additional effect)	-	0.21	0.21
Motivation at school aged 16	0.13	0.06	0.19
c.3: Qualifications			
Qualifications at 16	0.13	0.10	0.23
Additional qualifications by age 33	0.25	-	0.25

For example, the influence of father's class throughout the period when the child is growing up works out at a combined standardised coefficient of (0.12+0.18+0.03+0.03) = 0.36, and the impact of parents' education (father and mother combined) is half as strong again (0.18). Parental aspirations throughout the period of childhood work out at a total coefficient of 0.17, and parental interest in the child's education (a factor derived from information about parents' school visits and teacher assessments of the level of parental interest) comes out at a total of 0.30. All of these factors are clearly important, but they are eclipsed by the combined effects of the two meritocracy factors. The total effect of ability works out at 0.85, and that of childhood ambition and effort comes out at 0.55.

Summarising all of this, we may say that, in predicting where people are likely to end up in the class system at age 33, their ability alone is well over twice as important as their class origins, three times more powerful than the degree of interest their parents showed in their schooling, and is five times more powerful than their parents' level of education or the aspirations which their parents harboured for them while they were growing up.

Table 15
Proportion of Variance in Occupational Prestige Scores at Age 33 explained by different categories of variables

CATEGORY	PROPORTION OF VARIANCE EXPLAINED
Social advantages/disadvantages:	
a1: Parents class	0.03
a2: Housing conditions	0.00 *
a3: Schooling	0.00 *
Parents' behaviour and attitudes:	
b1: Aspirations for child	0.01
b2: Interest in child's education	0.03
Individual characteristics:	
c1: Academic ability	0.17
c2: Ambition	0.05
c3: Qualifications	0.06
TOTAL VARIANCE EXPLAINED	0.35

Note: * Less than 0.01

This is confirmed by Table 15, which summarises the proportion of the variance in occupational status at age 33 which is explained by the various factors and variables in the path model. The model has accounted for around 35 per cent of the variance in occupational prestige scores.[13] Fully half of this is explained by ability alone. Motivation accounts for a further five per cent, qualifications for six per cent, and class origins for just three per cent. Of all the variables and factors we have been able to measure, ability is by far the most important.

To put this another way, if you had to bet on which social class a child born in 1958 would end up in, and you could ask for just one item of information to help with your prediction, the information you would want would not be the parents' social class, nor the type of school the child went to, nor even the degree of support and encouragement the child received from its parents as it was growing up. The information you would want would be the child's IQ test result at age 11.

This suggests that sociologists have for many years been barking up the wrong tree. If we are interested in identifying those factors which play the most important role in determining social mobility, then we should be paying far more attention to factors to do with individuals themselves—especially their ability and their motivation—and worrying much less about the social advantages and disadvantages associated with the class they are born into. It does make some difference whether your father is an unskilled manual worker or a well-paid professional, whether your mother left school at the minimum legal age or stayed on to do exams, whether your parents encouraged you in your school work or showed no interest in your education, whether you attended a private school or a state comprehensive, whether you had your own bedroom in which to do your homework or had to share with a sibling. But in the end, what matters far more is whether you are bright, and whether you work hard.

The evidence reviewed in this chapter strongly suggests that people in Britain are getting allocated to occupational class positions mainly according to meritocratic principles.

Sociologists and others who say they want to improve children's life chances should therefore be thinking less about income redistribution and shutting down private schools, and more about how to raise the cognitive ability and/or level of motivation of those at the bottom. We shall return to this issue in Chapter VII.

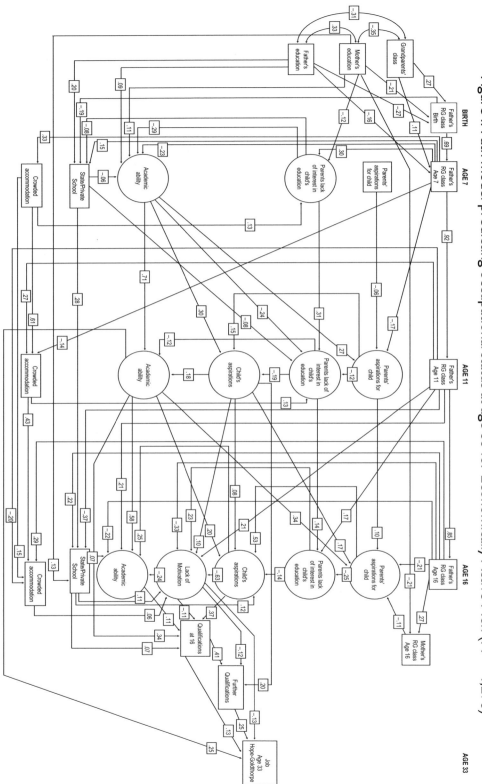

Figure I: Path model predicting occupational status at age 33 for Economically Active Men (N = 4,298)

6

How Robust are the Research Findings?

In the last two chapters we have seen:

- Goldthorpe's original findings on relative social mobility rates, which he interpreted as evidence of 'gross' inequalities of opportunity between the classes, are in fact consistent with a model of meritocratic recruitment. The only part of Goldthorpe's data matrix which does not fit the model is middle class downward mobility, which is about 25 per cent less common than it should be under purely meritocratic conditions.

- The NCDS longitudinal panel survey of children born in 1958 shows clearly that ability (measured by an IQ test at age 11) correlates more strongly with class of destination than with class of origin; that ability and motivation are the key predictors of lower working class success and of middle class failure; that low ability does not necessarily prevent entry into the middle class (not even for children from lower class backgrounds), but high ability does tend to safeguard individuals against ending up in the semi- and unskilled manual working class; and that social mobility disparity ratios comparing class I/II origins with class IV/V origins are roughly halved once ability differentials between the classes are taken into account.

- Many of the factors which have attracted the attention and concern of sociologists down the years—private schooling, parental support, material conditions in the home, the 'cultural capital' passed on by middle class parents—turn out, even when statistically significant, to exert only relatively minor effects on people's class destinations. Factors which sociologists have generally ignored or dismissed as 'ideological'—IQ and hard work—turn out to be much more important. Cognitive ability is more than twice as important as class origins in influencing occupational outcomes. Half of the explained variance in occupational outcomes at age 33 can be explained by cognitive ability alone.

The compelling conclusion to be drawn from all of this is that, while not everybody in the middle class 'deserves' to be there judged on their talent and effort alone, people who have ability and who work hard generally succeed. To the extent that the system falls short of the meritocratic ideal, it is not in blocking talented working class children from rising, but is in protecting dull middle class children from falling.

This is not, however, a conclusion many prominent British academics working in this field are even now willing to endorse. Nor is it reflected in the various reports on social mobility which the government has been publishing in recent years. The SAD thesis continues to dominate both the academic and public policy agendas as if this contrary evidence had never been assembled. So is there something wrong with the evidence I have been outlining? Is there something awry with my analysis, something fishy about my findings?

We can consider this possibility in two ways. First, we can look at the criticisms which have been made against my work by those who claim my conclusions are wrong. Secondly, we can look at other people's research findings, published since I completed this work, to see whether they are consistent with what I have been arguing. In both cases, my analysis stands up remarkably well. In fact, the key arguments come out of this examination stronger than before.

Incompetent, ignorant and biased?

My suggestion that ability and effort generally count for more than class background in explaining why people end up in the jobs that they do has provoked strong criticism from various sociologists concerned to defend the SAD thesis,[1] but the most combative rebuttal has come, predictably, from John Goldthorpe.[2] Writing jointly with Richard Breen, he not only claims that I am wrong, but he attempts to demolish my academic credibility by suggesting that I am also incompetent, biased and ill-read.[3]

The first point to note about this attack is that Goldthorpe and Breen (let us call them GaB) simply ignore my discovery that Goldthorpe's own mobility data are almost perfectly consistent with what we would expect to find in a meritocratic system. When pushed, they say this has 'no relevance' to the debate.[4] Yet it is hugely relevant.

In his original work, Goldthorpe confidently asserted that odds ratios of the magnitude he was reporting *could not* be explained by differences in people's abilities, but must rather be 'presumed' to derive from 'inequalities of opportunity that are rooted in the class structure'.[5] My model of mobility under perfectly meritocratic conditions shows this 'presumption' was false, for to a remarkable degree, these odds ratios can be predicted from class-based IQ differences. It was therefore illegitimate to assume, as Goldthorpe had done (and as later commentators and analysts have continued to do), that unequal outcomes necessarily signify the existence of class-based inequalities of opportunity. This is a crucial issue, but GaB completely duck it.

Instead, they focus on my analysis of the NCDS data. One of their complaints is that my work is 'partial' and 'unjustified' because I emphasise disparity ratios rather than odds ratios. They say I do this because I want to focus on upward mobility rates (which tend to be high) to the neglect of downward mobility rates (which tend to be lower).[6] This charge is easily rebutted, for I have consistently drawn attention to the 'stickiness' of middle-class downward mobility rates, identifying this as the principal weakness in the meritocracy thesis, and I have never attempted to 'hide' this finding.

GaB go on to claim I am 'incompetent' because of the way I measure key variables, in particular 'social class'. Like thousands of researchers before me, I relied mainly on the class schema favoured by the government's Office of Population Censuses and Surveys (OPCS), rather than the one developed by Goldthorpe. GaB take offence at this, arguing that my analysis is less 'refined' than theirs.[7] They also criticize my treatment of class as a single interval variable, suggesting that this has 'blunted' its potential explanatory power in my models. Instead, they say class should be entered into these models as a series of discrete 'dummy variables'.[8]

We can deal with these criticisms very easily by re-running the regression models from the previous chapter, defining variables as GaB want them defined, and building the models in a manner as favourable as possible to their SAD thesis. The result is set out in Table 16. This uses Goldthorpe's own social class schema, analyses class as a series of discrete dummy variables as GaB demand, and uses the NCDS ability and motivation measures that GaB prefer (even though these are cruder than the ones used in my path model).[9]

Because GaB also worry that class might not be measured as precisely as ability (in which case it will not perform as powerfully in regression modelling), we can try to compensate for this possibility by (a) forcing our model to include a range of other 'social background' measures (so aspects of class advantage and disadvantage that are not picked up by the class variables can still be detected by other indicators), and (b) by giving the SAD variables the maximum possible explanatory advantage when we construct the model by entering them first. Thus, in Table 16, the 'class of origin' dummy variables have been entered at the first step, so their potential explanatory power is maximized, and all the other variables which might point to the importance of middle-class advantages or working-class disadvantages have been entered next. Given these procedures, it is difficult to see how class effects could be said to be under-estimated in this model. Ability and motivation (the merit variables) have been held back to the third step (even though they correlate with class destination more strongly than the SAD variables), following which the model is completed by the qualifications which people have accumulated at school and later in life.

The importance of the order of variable entry in least squares regression

The regression models presented in Tables 12 and 13 were developed in an exploratory 'stepwise' manner, allowing the order in which variables were entered to be determined by the strength of their association with the dependent variable. Because IQ scores correlate with class destination more strongly than class or origin does, ability was entered before class in these models.

Variables entered first in a multiple regression can, however, appear stronger than they really are, for they can claim all the variance that they share with other variables which are not entered until later. To ensure that the SAD hypothesis gets all the help we can possibly give it, we can therefore force the weaker SAD variables to enter the model first so they can soak up all available shared variance.

There are three sets of information to consider in Table 16. The first is the relative size of the Beta coefficients. At step 3, ability (0.26) and motivation (0.14) far outweigh any of the other variables entered at earlier stages, even though they are handicapped by late entry, and at step 4, ability (0.16) in particular is still having a substantial effect, even after school and post-school qualifications are taken into account. All this reinforces my earlier results which found that ability and motivation have much larger standardised coefficients than any of the SAD variables, and that they continue to exert a relatively large effect even when qualifications are added to the model.

Table 16
Building a regression model as favourable as possible to the SAD thesis[10]

| | Standardised Beta Coefficients: | | | |
	MODEL 1	MODEL 2	MODEL 3	MODEL 4
Class origins				
Father class I	0.270***	0.165***	0.118***	0.081***
Father class II	0.148***	0.087***	0.055***	0.038**
Father class III	0.100***	0.066***	0.040**	0.022
Father class VI	0.180***	0.115***	0.083***	0.065***
Father class V	0.076***	0.056***	0.038**	0.028*
Father class VI	0.064***	0.051**	0.031*	0.019
Other social advantages/disadvantages:				
Parents' education		0.148***	0.092***	0.049***
Parental contact with school		0.066***	0.024*	0.020
Parents read to child age 7		0.043***	0.030**	0.013
Overcrowding in parental home		0.054***	0.027*	0.020
Home lacked basic amenities		0.019	0.011	0.005
Pre-school education		0.011	0.011	0.009
Private education		0.035**	0.038**	0.023*
Ability plus effort:				
Ability test score, age 11			0.262***	0.157 ***
Motivation score, age 16			0.143***	0.076***
Qualifications:				
School exam results				0.140***
Post-school qualifications				0.260***
CUMULATIVE ADJ R²:	0.065	0.103	0.193	0.273

The second set of information to take from Table 16 relates to the significance levels (designated by asterisks: * <0.05, ** <0.01, *** <0.001). With a sample size of 6,795, it is not difficult for a variable to achieve a 'statistically significant' effect, and we should probably discount anything above 0.01, and perhaps even insist on a level of 0.001 or lower. Inspecting model 3, we see that both ability and motivation achieve significance at this highest level, as do three of the class of origin variables (classes I, II and IV) and the measure of parental education. This pattern continues once qualifications are included (model 4), although the significance of class II membership now becomes marginal.

All this confirms that ability and motivation have a significant independent effect on people's class destinies, as do qualifications. Parents' level of education is also important, and if the father is a member of the service class (particularly the 'upper' service class), or if he is a self-employed small businessman (class IV), then class origins also play a significant part in influencing class destinations. This is not, however, true of any other class background, and this reinforces my earlier argument that class origins have their main effect through the ability of middle-class parents to prevent their children from sliding downwards. Knowing whether or not somebody has working class origins simply does not help us predict where they end up at age 33.

The third, and most important, information to be taken from Table 16 concerns the change in the adjusted R^2 as we move from Model 1 to Model 4. We see from this that class origins, defined and measured as Goldthorpe wants them to be, explain *at most* just seven per cent of the variance in occupational destinations at age 33. Adding other measures of socially advantaged or disadvantaged backgrounds raises this to 10 per cent. When we then add the ability test scores at age 11 and motivation at age 16, the total proportion of variance explained almost doubles, to 19 per cent, and when qualifications are added, we can raise this again, to 27 per cent.[11] Class origins thus account *at most* for a quarter of the explained variance in class destinations, while ability and motivation account for *at least* one-third, and ability, motivation and qualifications together account for *at least* 62 per cent.

Yet GaB are still unimpressed! Responding to this re-analysis, they simply reject what they call my 'variable race' between SAD and merit measures. Rather than developing models which can assess the relative explanatory strength of SAD and merit variables, they prefer to subject only the meritocracy thesis to empirical test and to leave the SAD thesis unchallenged. The way they do this is to measure the degree to which class of origin/class of destination odds ratios change when ability and motivation are taken into account.

Comparing class I and class VII origins and destinations, they report that odds ratios fall from 20.7 to 11.1 for men (a drop of 46 per cent), and from 16.3 to 6.3 for women (a drop of 61 per cent) when merit variables (the ability test results at 11 and the motivation score at 16) are added. When qualifications (measured by a single variable) are also added, odds ratios fall further still (they do not report the figures, but from their data I calculate them to be just 7.4 for men and 3.3 for women—representing additional falls of 33 and 48 per cent respectively).[12]

GaB think these results disprove the meritocracy thesis because 'inequality is far from eliminated when "merit" variables are brought into the analysis'.[13] But this is disingenuous. Nobody ever claimed occupational placement was *completely* driven by ability and hard work. Of course other factors (including parenting and home background) will have *some* influence on how people grow up. For Goldthorpe to reject the meritocracy hypothesis because it fails to explain the *entire* association between class origins and destinations is like saying that the link between smoking and lung cancer is disproved if we find some smokers do not get the disease while some non-smokers do, or that the hypothesis of man-made global warming is disproved if we discover that sunspot activity also affects the world's climate.

The reductions GaB report in their odds ratios actually point to the same sort of conclusion as that derived from my regression models and path model—that ability and motivation are the principal drivers of class mobility. Table 17 summarises all these different models. It shows that 'merit variables' account for at least one-third (and probably half) of the explained variance in class destinations, and that when qualifications are added,[14] the proportion of variance explained increases to as much as two-thirds. It also shows that merit variables halve the size of the most extreme odds ratios (and again, adding qualifications reduces odds ratios even further, by about two-thirds). Breen and Goldthorpe's work looks broadly consistent with mine in that both show that 'merit' makes a huge dent in the effect that social advantages and disadvantages have on people's class destinations. Goldthorpe still resists this conclusion, but other sociologists who have criticised my work in the past now broadly concur with it.[15]

Table 17
Estimates of relative strength of SAD and meritocracy variables[16]

	Regression model (class effect maximized)	Regression model (merit effect maximized)	Path model	Breen & Goldthorpe model
	% of total explained variance	% of total explained variance	% of total explained variance	% reduction in odds ratios
Class origin	24	4	9	Not estimated
Other SAD factors	14	1	11	Not estimated
Ability & effort	33	57	63	*Men:* 46 *Women:* 61
Qualifications	29	37	17	*Men:* 33 *Women:* 48

Support from later findings

The best test of the reliability of any social scientific finding is replication. Is the same result reproduced by different researchers working independently of each other on different data sets?

In this case, it has been. Apparently in complete ignorance of my debate with Goldthorpe, David Nettle, from the Open University's Department of Psychology and Biological Sciences, published a paper in 2003 in which he investigated the importance of cognitive ability in influencing class mobility among NCDS participants when they reached 42 years of age (nine years on from when I had studied them).[17] Using the OPCS five-class schema, he found that 60 per cent of the men in the sample now occupied a different class position from the one their fathers occupied, and the correlation between class of origin and class of destination was just 0.26. More importantly, he also showed that cognitive ability, measured by ability test scores at age 11, was still the key factor explaining upward and downward mobility. After taking test scores into account, the correlation between fathers' and sons' class locations fell to just 0.16.

Nettle reported that high intelligence increases the probability of occupational success right across the class system (i.e. the higher the IQ, the greater the likelihood of occupational success, irrespective of the class these men were born into). He also found that men who move into a higher class do not have higher IQs than those already there (this has also been reported in other studies, and it would seem to undermine Goldthorpe's claim that working class children have to 'show more merit' than middle class children to reach the same occupational level).[18] Nettle concluded: 'Intelligence is the strongest single factor causing class mobility in contemporary societies that has been identified.'[19]

Nettle's is not the only study to reach this conclusion. Leon Feinstein has looked at the relative significance of class background and cognitive ability for the earnings, qualifications and risk of unemployment of the 1970 birth cohort by the time they reached age 26.[20] He finds that reading and maths scores at age 10 are the best predictor of qualifications achieved by age 26, even after controlling for parental class, parental education, parental income and parental interest in education. Unemployment at age 26 is also strongly predicted by the age 10 maths score. Running an ordinary least squares regression to predict earnings, Feinstein finds, not only that reading and maths scores are strong predictors, but that fathers' class and qualifications are not statistically significant when entered as controls. While people with higher qualifications tend to earn higher wages, the results also show that ability (measured by the age 10 scores) has an additional effect on earnings, over and above its link to qualifications. Bright people, in other words, tend to earn more, even after their superior qualifications are taken into account.

Sophie von Stumm and her colleagues have also investigated the 1970 birth cohort, but she focuses on males when they reach the age of 30. By this time, 39 per cent of the panel members had moved up relative to their fathers' class and 27 per cent had moved down. The authors find that 'intelligence predicted class attainments to a far greater extent than social class of origin'.[21]

Is the importance of IQ declining?

We saw in Chapter 3 that some economists who have compared the 1958 and 1970 cohorts believe that income mobility fell between the two studies. They claim this is because the middle class took more advantage of the expansion of university places that occurred towards the end of the century. Because less intelligent middle class children went to university in greater numbers, they say the link between IQ and educational attainment has been weakened, and that British society has therefore become less meritocratic.[22]

There are three points to note about these findings.

The first is that (as we saw in chapter III), the 'decline' in income mobility may be an illusion, so the fall in the strength of the association between income and IQ may be illusory too. Ingrid Schoon compares the two cohorts looking at their class, rather than income, destinations and reports no change in the correlation with cognitive ability scores (r = 0.35 [1958 males]; 0.35 [1970 males]; 0.31 [1958 females]; 0.30 [1970 females]). She concludes: 'The processes influencing status attainment have remained more or less the same.'[23]

Secondly, the fall in the association between IQ and educational attainment following the expansion of higher education need not signify any weakening of meritocracy. Reflecting on a similar pattern in Australia, Gary Marks and Julie McMillan point out that, as university participation by high ability students approaches saturation (for not all high IQ students will want to go to university), further expansion of places will attract a more varied ability group, so the explanatory power of IQ should be expected to fall.[24]

The same effect may also occur as a result of the expansion of schooling. In 1960, only 12 per cent of British children stayed at school past the compulsory age, whereas now it is 70 per cent. This has increased qualification levels among lower ability children from all social backgrounds, thereby depressing the association between IQ and school success (in the 1958 cohort, 24 per cent of low IQ children from low income families passed 'O' levels, compared with 33 per cent of low IQ children from high income backgrounds; in the 1970 cohort, these proportions increased to 43 per cent and 60 per cent respectively). Discussing this change, Galindo-Rueda and Vignoles note, 'Ability became less important partly because the educational achievement of the least able students increased.'[25]

Thirdly, even if educational expansion has made IQ less important, intelligence still far outweighs class background in determining educational attainment. Stephen Machin and Anna Vignoles, for example, show that in the 1958 birth cohort, only one per cent of low ability boys from high income families got a university degree.[26] With the expansion of higher education, this proportion rose to eight per cent in the 1970 cohort. The authors point to this increase as evidence of how the middle class benefited from higher education expansion. But compare this with the figures for high IQ boys from low income families, 35 per cent of whom got degrees in the 1958 cohort, and 43 per cent in the 1970 cohort. Clearly, whether or not the middle class benefited disproportionately from the expansion of the universities, the real story here is that in both cohorts, IQ still convincingly trumps class in governing university entry.

Working with a different set of researchers, von Stumm has also analysed the class destinations achieved by a sample of twelve thousand Aberdeen boys born in the years 1950-1956 who completed four mental ability tests when they were 11 years of age. They were followed up when they were aged between 46 and 51, when their careers were approaching maturity. A path model was constructed which accounted for 48 per cent of the variance in class destinations—a strong model—and again, intelligence was the key explanatory variable. The ability test scores of these boys were twice as strong as their social class origins in predicting their educational achievements, and were almost twice as strong in predicting their class position in middle age.

Another Scottish study which extends over an even longer period in subjects' lives is reported by Ian Deary and his team.[27] They report on 243 men who were born in 1921, tested in 1932, and were then re-interviewed in the 1970s. Clearly, this study cannot tell us much about contemporary social mobility rates, but it is interesting for what it reveals about the link between intelligence and social class attainment over a lifetime. Its key finding is that these men were sifted and sorted throughout their lives, not according to their class origins, but on the basis of their IQs. The sample size is too small to say much about the link between IQ and downward mobility (due to the relatively small rate of downward movement), but the association between a high IQ and upward mobility is very clear. Men from class IV/V origins who made it to class I/II had average IQ scores of 110, whereas those who remained in class IV/V had average scores of just 94. Similarly, those from the skilled manual working class (class IIIM) who rose to class I/II had average IQ scores of 113 while those who remained in class IIIM had average scores of 98.

The authors of this study note that the association between IQ and class attainment was much stronger when these men reached middle age than when they were young and entering their first jobs. This reminds us that social mobility is intra- as well as inter-generational. Given that considerable movement continues to occur later in life, and that ability continues to influence occupational attainment even after completing education, studies which analyse class destinations when people are still only in their twenties or thirties are almost certainly under-estimating the link between IQ and eventual class destinations.

Deary also shows that the influence of IQ on class destinations is strongest for more intelligent people.[28] In other words, individuals who score highly on ability tests generally end up in higher class locations, but those who score poorly do not necessarily end up in lower class locations. This finding reinforces my own earlier results from the NCDS, where I showed that bright working class children can expect to succeed, but dull middle class children will not necessarily fail (their parents may find ways of protecting their future status, by buying them a better education, passing on business assets, and so on).

Not only has recent research confirmed that IQ is the major driver of educational and occupational success; it has also demonstrated that IQ is transmitted across the generations from parents to their children. Fernando Galindo-Rueda and Anna Vignoles analyse the maths and reading scores of children born to parents in the 1958 birth cohort study whose own cognitive ability was documented when they were young. They find 'strong ability transmission effects from parents to their offspring'. They note that parents' qualifications have some additional effect on children's reading scores, and they emphasise that 'social class effects on children's attainment are not removed completely' when parental ability is taken into account. But their conclusion is clear: the ability scores of parents when they were seven and 11 years of age correlate strongly and significantly with the scores achieved by their children when they reach seven, a result which the authors describe as 'remarkable'.[29]

There are now literally dozens of studies which show that IQ is an important influence on people's educational and occupational attainment, that it is to a significant extent inherited from their parents, and that it is a more important influence on their class destinations than their class origins are. A 'meta-analysis' conducted by Tarmo Strenze in 2006 included 49 different longitudinal studies from around the world and found that 'intelligence is a better predictor of success' than either parental class or qualifications.[30] None of this means that intelligence is the sole explanation for where people end up in life. But it does mean that explanations for social mobility that fail to take account of class-based IQ differences should be regarded as partial, biased and incomplete. [31]

What about effort?

Recent research has not only demonstrated the importance of cognitive ability in shaping people's occupational destinies. It has also begun to investigate in more depth the second string to the meritocracy bow — the importance of motivation, or how hard people work.

Psychologists have developed sophisticated techniques for measuring character traits like 'application' (the ability to stick at a task), 'self-regulation' (control over one's own emotions) and 'locus of control' (the belief that you can influence your own destiny), and they have found (a) that many of these characteristics typically vary according to the social class of one's parents, and (b) that they can be crucial in influencing educational and occupational success.

Feinstein's work, discussed above, shows that ability in childhood is quite strongly associated with 'attentiveness' and 'locus of control', but personality variables like these also turn out to have their own, independent influence on the achievement of qualifications and a higher income in adulthood. Similarly, 'anti-social behaviour' at a young age is associated with higher unemployment later on (those with high anti-social scores tend to find jobs, but then lose them). The crucial point about all these attributes is that they are associated with the social class of parents. Feinstein concludes that, to the extent that class is inter-generationally transmitted, a crucial element in the explanation may lie in parenting.

This is supported to some extent by von Stumm's analysis of the 1970 birth cohort when they reached 30. She confirms that positive

---

personality attributes do tend to vary with the social class of parents, and they can influence the income and occupational status attained later by the children. However, she insists that IQ is the crucial factor in all this, for bright children tend to become more confident and they behave better in the classroom. Positive behavioural attributes thus reinforce intelligence in boosting later educational and occupational prospects.[32]

Recently, the left-leaning think tank, Demos, investigated the importance of what it called 'character capabilities' for social mobility.[33] It noted that 'application', 'self-regulation' and 'empathy' all help predict educational and occupational success, and it found that these traits varied among five year-olds in the Millenium Cohort Study according to the social class of their parents. However, the crucial mediating factor was the style of parenting. Children whose parents link affection with a structured environment—what the report called 'tough love'—tend to develop the positive traits most strongly, while those whose parents are 'disengaged' develop them least successfully.

The Demos report suggests that targeted interventions at a very early age might be able to change the parenting practices of lower class parents, thereby strengthening the pro-success character attributes in their children. This is echoed by another left-of-centre think tank, the Institute of Public Policy Research (IPPR), which argues that quality of parenting far outweighs both income and social class of parents in influencing children's destinies. IPPR cites research suggesting that parental involvement is more than 4 times as important as social class in shaping children's educational outcomes at 16, and it believes that, 'Where parents in lower social classes are able to provide a high quality home environment, this can to a large extent overcome the disadvantages of living in a low income family.'[34]

The policy implications of all this are addressed in chapter VII.

7

Policy Responses:
Faint Hopes, False Starts and Red Herrings

We might have expected, given the weight of evidence we have been reviewing, that official government-sponsored research into social mobility in Britain would by now routinely take account of the role that differences of intelligence play in explaining class differences in educational and occupational achievement. Unfortunately, this is not the case.

It is depressing to report that *none* of the work reviewed in the last chapter linking class and intelligence to social mobility rates is addressed in *any* of the major reports on social mobility that have been coming out from government departments over the last two years. Three main reports have been issued; only one of them even mentions the word 'intelligence', and none discusses 'IQ':

- The Cabinet Office report, *Getting On, Getting Ahead (2008)*, was commissioned by Labour Prime Minister, Gordon Brown, to report on social mobility. It speaks of the need to allow people to 'realise their potential',[1] but it completely avoids the question of how this 'potential' is distributed across the social classes. Implicitly, it assumes an even distribution from the top to the bottom of the class system, for it follows Goldthorpe in defining 'perfect mobility' as the absence of any statistical association between origins and destinations (i.e. zero odds ratios). It then contrasts this ideal with evidence of what it calls 'large and systematic differences in outcomes, which start emerging at very young ages'.[2] These different outcomes are assumed to be the product of social inequalities, and the report devotes much of its attention to the influence on life chances of things like child care, schooling, training, parenting, family finances and neighbourhood effects. Differences of intelligence are never mentioned.

- The 'Milburn report' on fair access to the professions, *Unleashing Aspiration (2009)*, states that 'individual success should reflect innate talent and ability'.[3] Unlike the other reports, it does mention intelligence, but having satisfied itself that intelligence does not *wholly* determine occupational destinations, it then proceeds to ignore it.[4] Instead, it concentrates on the social advantages and disadvantages which it thinks determine people's life chances: maternal health, child poverty, early years care, parenting styles, 'cultural capital', 'social capital' (networks and contacts), ownership of family assets, time spent in education, qualifications, and job opportunities. This whole-hearted commitment to the SAD thesis is then reinforced by the dubious claim that Britain has lower social mobility rates than other comparable countries, which is said to be due to the greater income inequalities in this country. This explanation allows a link to be drawn between the 'old Labour' preoccupation with income redistribution and the 'new Labour' focus on increasing mobility rates, for it suggests that mobility cannot be increased without reducing income inequalities.

- The National Equality Panel report, *An Anatomy of Economic Inequality in the UK (2010)*, also ties the social mobility agenda to income redistribution. Like the other two reports, this one emphasises social advantages and disadvantages and ignores intelligence as a driver of class recruitment. It does recognise that cognitive ability test scores vary from a very young age between children from different socio-economic backgrounds, but it never addresses the possibility that this is because more intelligent people who gravitate to higher social classes tend to produce more intelligent offspring. Rather, it treats cognitive differences as reflections of class advantages and disadvantages. Children's test scores at age five, for example, are shown to reflect their mothers' level of educational attainment.[5] But this association is treated as evidence of educated parents passing on 'cultural capital' to their children, rather than a sign of cognitive transmission (intelligent mothers producing intelligent children), even though the latter interpretation is strongly supported by other research.[6] Like Goldthorpe thirty years ago, the report assumes that evidence of unequal outcomes is enough to demonstrate that the competition must have been unfair: 'The systematic nature of many of the differences we present... make it hard... to suggest that there is... equality of opportunity, however defined.'[7]

The lack in all three of these reports of any serious attempt to take account of intelligence differences is breathtaking. They all pay lip service to the meritocratic ideal—the principle that talent and hard work should determine individual success—yet none of them is interested in tracing the distribution of 'talent' within the population. Located firmly within the decades-old tradition of the SAD thesis, all three reports assume that when people from different class backgrounds perform differently, this must be due to the social advantages or disadvantages that they have experienced.

Now, it might be argued that there is no point in government reports acknowledging class-based differences of intelligence if these differences cannot easily be altered by public policy interventions. It makes more sense for politicians to concentrate on the social advantages and disadvantages which can be changed—things like improving access to university, extending the availability of training, or stretching the school leaving age. Perhaps in ignoring intelligence, these reports are just being practical?

There are two things wrong with this attempted justification. The first is that there *are* things public policy might do to raise the IQ scores of children from disadvantaged backgrounds, but this will not happen for as long as policy-makers refuse even to acknowledge that IQ is crucial, and that it varies by class.[8] The second is that, by ignoring intelligence, current thinking is in danger of spawning policies that will not work, and which might even make things worse. The basic point is this: we cannot hope to develop good policies if we ignore the key influence on the phenomenon we are hoping to change.

The policies that are being advocated and adopted at the current time fall into five main categories. The first four (education reform, job creation, positive discrimination and income redistribution) are all almost certainly doomed to fail, but this will not deter politicians from spending vast amounts of our money on them. The fifth (selective early intervention in parenting) might have some hope of modest success, insofar as it is able to boost the 'ability' and 'effort' displayed by lower class children. Let us consider each in turn.

1. Education, education, education...

We have seen that the years people spend in education, and the qualifications they achieve, both correlate strongly with the status and remuneration of the jobs they end up getting. Politicians and their advisers have responded to this by seeking to increase education and training as a way of expanding social mobility.

But what is true for individuals is not necessarily true for a whole society. If I get more qualifications than you do, I will be at an advantage when it comes to finding a 'good job'. But if we all get more qualifications, none of us will be any better placed in the competition for jobs than we were before. Instead, four things will happen:

- less intelligent children will get pushed into taking courses for which they are ill-suited;[9]

- academic standards will be diluted to allow more candidates to pass exams (so-called 'grade inflation');[10]

- the relative value of the qualifications people get will fall as more people achieve them;

- employers will ratchet up the level of qualifications they require from applicants in order to sort the sheep from the goats.

All of this has been happening in Britain for at least 20 years.

Educational qualifications have become what economists call 'positional goods'. A 'positional good' is one whose utility declines, the more people who gain access to it.[11] When only 5 per cent of the population had university degrees, for example, a degree was a powerful passport to career success. But when almost half of the population goes to university, a degree becomes commonplace. You may be disadvantaged if you do not have one, but the advantages of being a graduate are severely dissipated.

Simply increasing the number of graduates, or the number of people passing A-levels, or the number of 16 year-olds staying on at school, or the number of training places on vocational courses, will therefore achieve little in the way of increasing people's chances of getting a high income or a middle class job. All it will do is devalue the qualifications and trigger a diploma race as people chase ever-higher qualifications in order to distinguish themselves from the mass of other potential applicants.

The government is not to be dissuaded from this course, however. Since Tony Blair declared 'education, education, education' to be his 'three' policy priorities in 1997, the real level of government spending on schools has almost doubled to more than £42 billion per year. Six hundred thousand more pupils now leave school each year with five GCSE passes at grades A* to C, A-level pass rates have risen every year for the last 29 years (27 per cent of papers now achieve an A grade), and 43 per cent of 18-30 year-olds (36 per cent of 18 year-olds) are now in higher education.[12]

The average educational standard of the population may or may not have improved as a result of all this expansion, but what seems certain is that there has been no significant impact on relative social mobility rates. As we saw in chapter III, economists have been studying children born in the 1990s, as well as the new 'Millenium' cohort, and they find that the association between parental income and predictors of later success, such as reading age or degree entry, has not changed relative to the correlations recorded for the 1970 birth cohort. They conclude that there will be 'little change in intergenerational income mobility for these children'.[13]

We can, in fact, be more bullish than this. The Swedish Marxist, Gosta Esping-Andersen, notes in a recent essay that decades of educational reform and expansion—not only in Britain, but throughout the western world—have done almost nothing to change social fluidity.[14] In Britain, we have destroyed the grammar schools in favour of comprehensives, weakened and sometimes abolished streaming and setting within schools, fiddled with the curriculum to make it less 'male, white and middle class', pumped extra resources into schools in 'deprived' areas, changed teaching methods, pushed up the school leaving age, inflated GCSE and A-level pass rates, boosted teacher salaries, dismantled the binary divide in higher education and massively expanded the number of university places—but relative social mobility rates have remained more-or-less constant throughout all these upheavals.

Esping-Andersen says this is true in most other countries too. Indeed, he shows it does not matter much whether countries have retained selective schooling or abolished it, nor even how much money their governments have spent on education, for none of this seems to have affected their social fluidity rates. He concludes that the cause of the intergenerational link between socioeconomic origins and destinations does not lie in the education system at all, but is established long before children start school. He concludes: 'We must abandon our faith in education policy as the great leveller.'[15]

But in this field of policy, nothing succeeds like failure. Half a century of educational reform has not made a dent on relative mobility rates, but rather than accept Esping-Andersen's logical conclusion, our politicians, civil servants and policy academics continue to produce reports and proposals advocating yet more educational tinkering in the hope that the next policy tweak will be the one that makes the difference.

In its advice to the Prime Minister, Gordon Brown, for example, the 2008 Cabinet Office report had no hesitation in advocating more qualifications as the strategy for raising mobility rates: 'To enable more people to move up into better jobs the UK's education system needs to ensure more children attain qualifications than have done in the past.'[16] Never mind that the huge expansion in qualified people has had no impact on social mobility rates up until now. Even more expansion is called for.

Similarly, Alan Milburn's report on entry into the professions contains dozens of detailed recommendations for expanding opportunities for children from less privileged backgrounds, including mentoring schemes, preferential loans, kite-marked internships, enhanced careers advice services, 'social mobility bonds' and even the establishment of army, navy and air force cadets in every state school (starting with the most disadvantaged ones).[17] Milburn's report recognises that formal qualifications can become positional goods, and it even acknowledges my argument to this effect in *Unequal But Fair?* (the only example of my work being cited in any of these reports). But then it ignores the problem, insisting that 'continuing investment and reform' are still the 'key' to creating a more 'mobile society'.[18]

But if demolishing the grammar schools, downgrading A-levels and turning the universities into a mass system of higher education has done nothing to increase upward social mobility, are we seriously to believe that replacing more old school buildings and marshalling army cadet forces in the playgrounds are going to make any difference?

2. Increase the size of the middle class

Since the First World War, relative mobility rates have remained roughly constant, but absolute mobility has increased dramatically. The reason for this lies in the technological changes (together with a huge increase in state sector employment) which created many new middle class jobs in this period. Through most of the twentieth century, each generation experienced greater upward social mobility than the last, mainly because there was more 'room at the top' for them to move into as the middle class expanded and the working class shrank.

This dramatic expansion in the size of the middle class is, however, now tailing off. In an important paper, Goldthorpe and Mills find that absolute rates of upward (and downward) mobility for men have flattened out since the 1970s as the steam has gone out of the middle class expansion.[19] There is no more absolute movement, up or down, for men today than there was in the 1980s. Absolute mobility for women is still increasing. There is still more 'room at the top' for women of this generation than there was for their mothers, so like the men in earlier generations, women still enjoy much greater upward than downward movement. But overall, the big shift in the occupational system from manual to mental labour appears to be behind us. The class that Goldthorpe calls the 'salariat' is not going to keep growing in the future at the rate at which it grew in the past.

This slow-down in the *embourgeoisement* of Britain underlines the fallacy in government policies which aim to promote more upward mobility through increased education and training. As Goldthorpe and Mills point out, if the middle class is going to remain roughly the same size in the future, increasing people's consumption of education can only result in increased numbers of 'over-qualified' people doing lower status jobs.[20] Far from creating greater contentment and social cohesion, as the government hopes, further expansion of qualifications looks like a recipe for heightened social discontent as people's expectations get raised but not fulfilled.

In some of the recent social mobility reports, there are signs that policy advisers dimly recognise this problem, and they are responding to it by looking for ways to re-inflate the size of the middle class balloon. The Cabinet Office report of 2008, for example, puts a lot of emphasis on 'creating more and better jobs', presumably in the hope that the twentieth century expansion of the middle class can be continued into the twenty-first.[21] The Milburn report similarly states: 'Between now and 2020 the economy will need up to seven million new professionals, with up to nine in ten of all new jobs likely to be in these sectors.'[22]

Much of this looks like wishful thinking, for we cannot all be middle class. Trevor Noble pointed out more than ten years ago that the trend to replace manual with mental labour has to slow down as the middle class becomes saturated.[23] We cannot 'grow the middle class' indefinitely. Similarly, in a paper with Michelle Jackson, John Goldthorpe warns: 'There is no policy route back to the structural conditions of the mid-twentieth century. The very substantial growth in demand for professional and managerial personnel that then occurred was created by an historic shift in the scale of public administration, of health, education and social welfare provision, and of industrial and commercial organization that could scarcely be repeated.'[24]

It may be that governments in the future will be able to squeeze a little more social mobility out of the tube by increasing still further the size of the public sector middle class. Well over a million new state sector jobs were created under Labour after 1997, and many of them were middle class (the bulk of them—four in every five—were also taken by women).[25] This state spending splurge helped delay the slowdown in overall mobility, and is probably largely responsible for the continuing rise in female upward mobility rates, but it can only offer a temporary respite. A drive to expand the public sector service class indefinitely into the future is clearly unsustainable, for this increase in the public sector payroll has been a major contributor to the huge budget deficit which the country now faces, and it will almost certainly have to be trimmed back in the future rather than rolled forward.

Noble predicts a big reduction in upward mobility into the middle class as its size stabilises. By 2050, he says, if current rates of 'class inheritance' continue, the middle class will be largely self-recruiting. Goldthorpe agrees. The only way Labour politicians in the future will be able to deliver on their promise to increase mobility, he says, will be to increase fluidity within the occupational system, for the shape of the system itself is not going to change dramatically from now on.

3. Discriminate against the children of the middle class

In the more stable, relatively unchanging, occupational class structure that seems to be emerging, fluidity will only increase if downward mobility increases in order to open up more space at the top. Goldthorpe complains that 'New Labour' fails to understand this. He says politicians are happy to talk about increasing upward mobility, but he doubts whether they have the stomach for promoting more downward mobility in order to make this possible.[26]

The 2001 Cabinet Office review of social mobility did in fact address this issue by drawing a distinction between 'weak' and 'strong' policies for promoting meritocracy. In the weak form, government focuses its attention on removing barriers to upward mobility (e.g. by increasing access to education). In the strong form, attention is also paid to 'positively reduc[ing] barriers to downward social mobility for dull middle class children' (e.g. by attacking rights of inheritance).[27] The review noted that politicians are likely to feel more comfortable pursuing the 'weak' rather than the 'strong' version of meritocracy, for taking privileges away from people creates tensions, resentment and political conflict.

All the evidence reviewed in earlier chapters tells us that enabling upward mobility (the weak strategy for promoting fluidity) has not really been a problem. Bright children who work hard have tended to rise up the system. They have not necessarily gone as far as their talents and efforts might have equipped them to go (for social disadvantages still play some part in shaping their occupational destinies), but by and large, they have been able to enter the middle class if that is where they were aiming.

Where meritocracy has been falling short is not on working class upward mobility; it is on middle class downward mobility. In Table 7, we saw that mobility rates in Goldthorpe's 1972 survey are almost exactly what they 'should' be if class recruitment were based solely on ability—except that middle class downward mobility is about 25 per cent less than the meritocracy model predicted. Similarly, our analysis of the NCDS data showed that, while bright people tend to end up in the middle class, dull people do not necessarily end up in the working class, and this has been confirmed in later research on other data sets by Ian Deary and others.

The 'problem', therefore, is that middle class downward mobility is 'sticky'. This may not have looked like a pressing problem while the middle class itself was getting bigger, for there was still plenty of opportunity for bright working class children to succeed. But if the size of the middle class is now stabilising, the ability of middle class parents to protect their 'undeserving' children from sliding down the snakes may start to create serious blockages in the opportunities for 'deserving' working class children to climb the ladders. The question, if this happens, is whether there is anything the government could, or even should, do to change things.

Some academics and pressure groups think there is. They are beginning to advocate policies explicitly designed to hinder middle class achievement. Some have even started talking about the circumstances under which it is permissible for the state to prevent parents from helping their children.[28] But as politicians and their advisers start to move hesitantly in this direction, the implications are huge, for it means using the power of the state, not to promote opportunities for citizens, but to stifle them. The state, in other words, is to be used as an explicit instrument of class discrimination.

Various proposals are on the table, and most of them involve changes to the education system:

- Because middle class parents buy houses in the catchment areas of the best state schools, there are moves to scrap parental choice of schools in favour of random allocation and lotteries to force middle class children into less successful state schools.[29]

- Because academic selection by ability results in middle class 'over-representation', there is support for abolishing academic streaming and setting in state schools to pull bright middle class children back closer to the norm.[30]

- Because parents who can afford it may seek to withdraw their children from the state system and educate them privately, this escape route has to be closed off by forcing up independent school fees, and/or reducing the right of independent schools to determine their own intake.[31]

- Because the huge expansion of higher education has not changed the class composition of students entering universities (and may even have favoured middle class children), the class backgrounds of applicants will have to be monitored, and financial pressure will be brought to bear on universities to reduce the number of students from private schools while boosting the number from lower class backgrounds.[32]

110

Proposals like these raise two core questions. First, will they work? We have seen that education reform in the past has delivered remarkably little change in social fluidity. It may be that depriving the middle classes of access to a good education will be more successful as a tool of social engineering than opening up access to the working class has been, although the fierce determination of many middle class parents to do the best for their children suggests this is unlikely. Force their children into bad state schools and they will respond by buying private tuition. Discriminate against them when they apply for higher education places and they will turn to America or Europe to secure a good degree from an overseas university.

The second, and even more important, question is: are such policies justified? The pursuit of meritocracy is desirable, but should it be an overriding objective? Critics have pointed to tensions and contra-dictions between meritocracy and other goals that might be equally or more desirable.[33] In this case, we have to ask whether the achievement of meritocracy is so important that it justifies removing the rights of parents to have a say in how their children are educated, undermining academic standards, and turning universities into instruments of ministerial whim. Perhaps the 'weak' version is as far as the state should go in pursuing the meritocratic ideal.

Policy ideas like these are in their infancy. But as the expansion of the middle class comes to an end, and the pressure on upward mobility intensifies, proposals like these are likely to surface with increasing regularity. Calls for explicit 'positive discrimination', in particular, have only just begun and seem certain to strengthen in future.[34] In this fevered atmosphere, politicians of all parties will need to clarify where they stand, for while almost everybody is willing to pay lip service to the meritocratic ideal, the real question will be how far they are willing to trample over other cherished values in order to attain it.

4. Flatten the income distribution (and abolish child poverty)

We have seen that both the Milburn and National Equality Panel reports claim that Britain is less mobile than most other western countries, and that this is because income inequalities here are more marked. They say that, in more unequal societies like ours, privileged groups fight more tenaciously to hold on to what they have, so fluidity is reduced. As the National Equality Panel explains: 'Intergenerational mobility appears lower in societies such as ours which are more unequal—moving up a ladder is harder if its rungs are further apart, and those who start higher up the ladder will, unsurprisingly, fight harder to make sure their children do not slip down it.'[35]

There are some obvious problems with this argument:

- If people near the top of more unequal societies fight harder to retain what they have, it should also follow that those near the bottom will fight harder to achieve what others have. If the incentives are stronger in more unequal systems where the rewards of success are greater, this should operate at the bottom as well as the top, which means inequality should boost mobility rates, not depress them. These reports reject the argument that incentives weaken as inequalities narrow (they argue that the willingness to take risks and work hard is just as widespread in more equal countries as in less equal ones). But they cannot have it both ways. Why should inequality motivate people with a lot of money to hang on to their privileges, but not motivate those with little money to try to improve their situation? It is a one-eyed logic to suggest that narrowing the income gap would promote social mobility rather than restrict it.

- The claim that Britain is a less mobile society than other comparable nations also has to be challenged. As we saw in Chapter I, Britain comes around the middle of the international rankings on relative occupational (or 'class') mobility rates, we perform rather well on educational mobility data, and the comparative statistics on income mobility rates are too unreliable to make any clear judgements. Even those economists who say our income mobility rates are low admit that 'there is a lot of uncertainty about the UK', and the error in the comparative income statistics means it is impossible to be sure how countries like Australia, France, Britain, Sweden and the USA rank against each other.[36] This is an extraordinarily flimsy evidence base on which to build a serious argument for more income redistribution.

- In a more unequal society, a small shift in one's relative position on the income distribution represents a bigger absolute move than in a less unequal society (precisely because the 'rungs on the ladder are further apart'). Because incomes are more dispersed in Britain than in, say, Scandinavia, a Brit doesn't have to move so far up the

112

income distribution in order to secure the same increase in income as a Swede. So even if it were true that greater income inequality correlates with lower income mobility rates, this would not necessarily mean that the opportunity to improve one's situation would be more limited.

- There is also the problem of spurious correlation in these reports. Gosta Esping-Andersen claims that relative class mobility in Sweden has been increasing over the last twenty years, but he links this to the introduction of universal child care rather than the narrower income distribution.[37] Their fondness for high taxes and generous welfare payments is not the only distinguishing feature of the Scandinavians.

We also have to consider how the desired compression of the income distribution would be brought about. The National Equality Panel talks of increasing the National Minimum Wage and encouraging 'asset-building' by council tenants, but it is clear that any serious attempt to compress incomes would have to be based on higher taxes on higher earners and/or more generous welfare transfers to non-employed households. Both of these policies could dampen mobility rather than increasing it, for higher taxes are likely to reduce the incentive to climb the ladder, while more generous welfare could make it easier to stay on the bottom rung. Even if these 'perverse incentive' effects did not materialise, it is difficult to see how egalitarian policies like these might increase social mobility rates.

In addition to advocating more income redistribution, these reports also link enhanced social mobility to the government's campaign to eradicate child poverty. Milburn, indeed, insists that, 'Unless child poverty is tackled, social mobility will be thwarted.'[38]

In reality, of course, 'eradicating child poverty' and 'increasing income redistribution' amount to much the same thing, for 'poverty', like inequality, is measured in relative income terms (the Labour Party says someone is 'in poverty' if their income, adjusted for household size, is below 60 per cent of the middle income in the distribution). The policies that might 'eradicate' child poverty (essentially, an increase in state transfers to families in the bottom quarter of the income distribution) are therefore much the same as those which would be adopted to reduce income inequality.

Indeed, as I have shown elsewhere, Labour's declared intention of eradicating child poverty can *only* be achieved through a huge increase in the generosity of state payments, for the great majority of households below the poverty line are full-time welfare recipients.[39] Again, therefore, we have to ask how giving people on benefits more welfare is likely to improve their children's career prospects.

It is true, as these reports say, that children growing up in homes below the poverty line are less likely to succeed, educationally and occupationally, than children reared by more affluent parents. But to deduce from this that their mobility chances would be enhanced simply by giving their parents more money is naive. Increasingly, research is finding that a major factor contributing to the disadvantage experienced by these children has to do with the way they are being brought up (bad parenting, family instability, and a lack of structure and support in their lives), rather than a lack of material resources. The quality of parenting is something governments might try to do something about, but it has little to do with lack of money.

Class, income and good parenting

In 2010, Labour's Equality minister, Harriet Harman, insisted: 'You can't separate out good parenting skills from family income. The two are so strongly correlated.'[40] But this confuses correlation with causation. It is true that 'good parenting' tends to vary by income and social class. But it does not follow from this that increasing people's income will improve their parenting skills, nor that improved parenting depends on giving families more money.

It is quite possible for low income parents to develop strong parenting skills, just as high income parents can be neglectful of their children. If the problem we are addressing is how to improve the way children are being brought up, the solution will lie in changing behaviours and attitudes—not in giving people more money.

---

5. Early intervention to strengthen character

As I noted at the start of this book, most of our evidence on social mobility is based on people who are employed. Economists' estimates of income mobility look only at earnings, so they exclude anyone without a job. Sociologists do include some jobless people in their 'social class' categories—spouses who are not employed, for example, are often given the occupational status of their employed partners, and retired and unemployed people may be classified on the basis of their most recent job—but this can blur the distinction between households which normally participate in paid work of some kind, and those which depend heavily and regularly on state benefits.

Although we now know a great deal about social mobility between the working class and the middle class, and between low earners and high earners, we therefore know very little about social mobility between those who work and those in the substratum of welfare-dependent households at the very bottom of our society. Either, the latter are excluded from mobility studies, or they get subsumed within bigger 'class' categories.

This 'group at the bottom' is hard to define precisely, although most observers agree they are there, and that their numbers have been increasing. David Goodhart talks of 'the long tail' of disillusioned, unqualified, jobless people who have been marginalised as a result of the decline in traditional manual, working class jobs.[41] The government talks of the problem of 'NEETS' (young people not in education, employment or training).[42] The European Union talks of people who are 'socially excluded' as a result of poverty, unemployment and lack of educational qualifications.[43] And Charles Murray talks of 'the growth of the underclass'.[44]

The defining characteristics of this substratum are hard to pin down, but we are talking about a group of people who are marginal to mainstream society. They are generally 'poor' and ill-educated, but 'poverty' is not what defines them. Murray focuses on three indicators (detachment from the labour force, criminality and lone motherhood), but there is an element of tautology in a behavioural definition which recognises the underclass by what it does. Alan Buckingham is more sociological, defining underclass membership by a combination of a weak employment record, residence in public rental housing, and long-term dependency on welfare. On these criteria, Buckingham estimates the size of the underclass at about five per cent of the UK population. He finds people in this situation tend to share certain behaviours, attitudes and character traits in common: a failure to develop long-term relationships, low IQ scores, a weak work ethic, and relatively high levels of criminality. He also shows that childhood behaviours and attitudes (e.g. truanting from school) are powerful predictors of an underclass destination.[45]

Although we do not know a lot about them, there is some work that has looked at mobility rates of people born into 'deprived' homes. Analysing the 1958 birth cohort, Paul Johnson and Howard Reed found that growing up in a household with an unemployed father roughly doubles a child's probability of becoming unemployed themselves. Nevertheless, more than four in five children with unemployed fathers avoided unemployment when they grew up, so intergenerational mobility out of unemployment is more a norm than an exception.[46]

Jo Blanden reports similar findings for children who grew up in households below the 'poverty line'. In the 1958 cohort, 19 per cent of the children of poor parents were poor at the age of 30, as compared with ten per cent of the children from non-poor households. Again, therefore, we find that children raised by disadvantaged parents are twice as likely to end up disadvantaged themselves, but four out of five of them somehow managed to avoid this fate. Looking at those who avoided poverty, Blanden notes an association with cognitive ability test scores at the age of five, and with the level of interest and encouragement shown by their parents as they were growing up.

This recognition of the role of parenting echoes some of the research findings discussed in Chapter VI, where we saw that psychological indicators like anxiety, self-esteem, hyper-activity and locus of control often correlate with the social class of one's parents and may exert a significant influence on educational and occupational performance. Recognition of this link between parental disadvantage, parenting style and children's eventual life chances is now beginning to influence policy thinking:

- A 2009 Demos report identifies 'character capabilities' as crucial influences on social mobility chances.[47] It finds that 'application', 'self-regulation' and 'empathy' all predict educational and occupational success, and it finds these traits tend to develop with different styles of parenting (children brought up with 'tough love' develop them most strongly, and those whose parents are 'disengaged' develop them least successfully). These parenting styles tend in turn to vary across social classes. The report concludes that targeted interventions at a very early age might be able to change the parenting practices of lower class parents, thereby strengthening the character attributes of their children.

- Another left-of-centre think tank, the Institute of Public Policy Research, argues that quality of parenting far outweighs both income and social class of parents in influencing children's destinies. It finds parental involvement is more than 4 times as important as social class in shaping children's educational outcomes at 16, and it believes that, 'Where parents in lower social classes are able to provide a high quality home environment, this can to a large extent overcome the disadvantages of living in a low income family.' Socialisation, it says, is the 'key factor in boosting life chances for those born into disadvantage'.[48]

It seems the left is belatedly rediscovering the importance of the nineteenth century concern with character building and moral improvement.[49]

It is not just personality that gets shaped by early parenting, of course. We saw in Chapter IV that up to 40 per cent of cognitive ability reflects environmental influences, and it seems likely that the key environmental influences occur as a result of parenting in early childhood. We have seen how ability scores tend to improve from the age of 42 months among low-scoring middle class children while they deteriorate among higher-scoring lower class children. Having said that, our path model (Fig. 1, p. 86) also showed that a child's ability might influence the parenting it receives—bright children, for example, elicit stronger interest and support from their parents than dull children.

Psychological research therefore points strongly to the importance of early years parenting in influencing children's later social mobility chances. The key character and ability attributes that will help shape their life chances are embedded in most children long before they start school.[50] But what can or should government do to influence this?

Two obvious strategies suggest themselves: government can try to improve parenting, and/or it can try to compensate for poor parenting by investing in high quality, early years child care outside the home. Either way, it makes sense to target the policy interventions on the families which need this help—there is not much point in spending public money providing parenting classes for good parents, or high

117

quality early years care for children who are already being well nurtured at home by parents who want to care for them.

One way of *improving parenting* might be to link receipt of government family payments to specified behaviours or outcomes. As I have noted elsewhere,[51] the rationale for giving parents family payments is that society requires and expects them to raise their children according to certain minimum standards, and it would not be inappropriate if payments were reduced or withheld in cases where parents do not meet these standards. In Mexico, cash payments for poor families require recipients to keep their children in school and to take them for regular health checks, and the result has been a marked improvement in school attendance and a fall in childhood malnutrition.[52] In Australia, receipt of the lump-sum maternity payment is conditional on having one's child vaccinated, and pilot programmes in remote Aboriginal communities (where there are serious problems of child abuse, drug taking and alcohol bingeing) have tied welfare and family payments to conditions around school attendance, child abuse and substance abuse.[53] In Britain in 2002, the Blair government proposed that Child Benefit should be forfeited by parents whose children were persistently truanting from school, but the proposal met with fierce resistance from lobby groups and was withdrawn. Perhaps it is time to try again.[54]

Minimum standards of parenting which are known to impact on children's wellbeing—things like regular school attendance, preventing children's involvement in anti-social or criminal behaviour, and avoiding their exposure to illegal drug use in the home—could be attached to parents' continuing receipt of family payments. Receipt of the Sure Start Maternity Grant could also be made conditional on attendance at parenting classes.[55]

Improved parenting might also be selectively reinforced by exposing children of inadequate parents to *high quality child care* from an early age. The Labour government actively increased access to child care for some years through the Sure Start programme, but its commitment is to universal provision. This has spread the resources thinly as integrated Children's Centres have been opened in localities across the country, and the middle classes have not been slow to avail themselves of the subsidies that are available. As a result, Sure Start today is as much about providing child care for middle class women who want to go back to work as it is about strengthening the upbringing of children from the most disadvantaged homes. This divided objective has arguably diluted its impact.

The Milburn report claims that, 'Early years care is beneficial for all children, the most disadvantaged especially. Continued investment here is important for social mobility.'[56] But in the first two or three years of life, there is no evidence that institutional child care helps the development of 'all children'. Well-adjusted children from loving and supportive homes can benefit as they get older, by interacting with other children and developing their social skills, but they gain little or nothing from earlier exposure to institutional care, and they can suffer (there is some evidence of a link, for example, between long hours spent in child care at an early age and later aggression and other behavioural problems).[57]

Milburn is right, however, that early exposure to good quality institutional care might help the development of children who are suffering from neglectful or inadequate parents, although even here, the evidence is not straight-forward. Child care does seem to boost the reading ages of these children, and it helps prepare them better for school, but most of the positive effects on cognitive development seem to fade after they start school, and there appears to be no long-term beneficial effect on their IQ scores.[58]

If it is true that limited-hours, good quality, child care for the under-threes can be beneficial for children who are not receiving good parenting, the policy dilemma then becomes how to target these children. One broad-brush approach would be to focus on families in long-term receipt of welfare benefits. It might be made a requirement of receipt of Income Support, for example, that parents claiming benefits should make themselves available for part-time work as soon as their youngest child is 12 months old. A free, part-time place would then be made available for the child in the local Sure Start Children's Centre, at the same time as the parent/s re-established their connection with the world of work.[59]

Challenging the myths

There is one more, simple thing government could and should do to support social mobility, and that is to stop telling people how hard it is to improve themselves. We do not live in a perfectly meritocratic society, and the playing field is not perfectly level. But this does not justify the bloated rhetoric, casual distortions and blatant untruths that routinely infiltrate public debate on this issue in Britain.

In the introduction to this book, I identified four pervasive 'social mobility myths' which too often go unchallenged as a result of the blanket of ideological orthodoxy which has settled over this field. In the course of the book, I have shown why these familiar claims should be challenged rather than uncritically accepted:

- *The myth that Britain is 'a closed shop society' in which life chances are heavily shaped by the class into which you are born.* It was absurd for Alan Milburn, in the preface to his 2009 report, to describe Britain as a 'closed shop society' when mobility is so common and widespread. Goldthorpe's original survey found that 49 per cent of sons ended up in a different class from their father (based on a three-class model), and his 1983 follow-up found that 53 per cent had changed classes. Heath and Payne show that, throughout the twentieth century, half or more of the population changed its class position relative to that of their fathers, so it has been more common for somebody to change classes than to stay put. In the 1958 birth cohort study, by the age of 33, 45 per cent of the men and 39 per cent of the women had moved upwards relative to the social class of their parents, and 27 per cent of the men and 37 per cent of the women had moved down. In the 1970 cohort (assessed at age 30), the equivalent figures were 42 per cent (men) and 41 per cent (women) moving up, and 30 per cent (men) and 35 per cent (women) moving down. And as people get older, mobility increases still further. This looks nothing like a 'closed shop society'. Nor is it true, as is commonly also suggested, that Britain is a significantly more 'closed' society than other western countries. It is not.

- *The myth that social mobility, already limited, is now getting worse.* It is not true that mobility has been falling, even though this is regularly repeated by politicians, policy makers and academics (the Conservatives have even claimed, ludicrously, that 'social mobility in Britain has ground to a halt').[60] Looking at class mobility, Erikson and Goldthorpe found that overall 'fluidity' has remained fairly constant over time, and if anything, this conclusion has been shown to be too pessimistic. Heath and Payne found fluidity has been increasing, and this was supported by Gershuny's analysis of the British Household Panel Study and by Lambert's long-term historical analyses. Although some economists claim to have found a fall in income mobility between the 1958 and 1970 birth cohorts, Goldthorpe and Jackson show there was very little change in class mobility, and Ermisch and Nicoletti report no significant change in income mobility rates for people born from between 1950 and 1972. It seems the economists may have been misled by unreliable data on parental incomes in the earlier survey. There are signs that rates of absolute upward mobility are now stabilising as the expansion of the middle class comes to an end, but what Goodhart calls 'the lazy consensus which has decreed the end of social mobility' is quite simply wrong.

- *The myth that differences of ability between individuals either do not exist, or are irrelevant in explaining their differential rates of success.* Ever since Goldthorpe illegitimately deduced the existence of unequal opportunities from evidence of unequal outcomes, academics and policy makers have been following the same faulty logic which ignores the link between class and intelligence. The 2001 Cabinet Office review wrongly claimed that a meritocratic society should entail 'the absence of any association between class origins and destinations'. The 2008 *Getting On, Getting Ahead* report similarly defined 'perfect mobility' as the absence of any statistical association between origins and destinations and cited 'large and systematic differences in outcomes' as evidence against the possibility of meritocratic selection. The 2009 Milburn report likewise insists that 'we would expect to see substantially more social mobility' if Britain really were a meritocracy, but it gives no justification for this assertion. And the 2010 National Equality Panel report appeals to 'the systematic nature of many of the differences' to deny the possibility of 'equality of opportunity, however defined'. None of these reports recognises that, in a meritocracy, cognitive ability *must* vary across social classes, which means that middle class children *should be expected* to achieve disproportionate success. When we take account of the distribution of intelligence, the 'strong associations' between class origins and destinations that so impress academics and policy makers suddenly become a lot weaker. Differences in average ability levels explain about half of the disparity in the relative chances of children from different backgrounds achieving different class destinations. Ability is well over twice as important as class origins in influencing class destinations, it is three times more powerful than parental interest and support, and five times more powerful than parental education. Fully half of the variance in class destinations is explained by ability alone, and class origins account *at most* for a quarter of it (even when models are deliberately set up to favour class-based explanations). All of these findings have been independently replicated many times over, yet official investigations into social mobility in this country continue, persistently, to ignore them.

- *The myth that governments can increase mobility via top-down social re-engineering within the education system and forcing more income redistribution.* The ideal of promoting social mobility by increasing meritocracy has in the last few years been used to justify some old-style socialist politics which in reality have little or nothing to do with increasing individual opportunities or rewarding effort and ability. Despite the fact that decades of radical educational reform have done little to change social fluidity, both the Milburn and National Equality Panel reports advocate more of the same. Although there is clear evidence that educational qualifications have become self-defeating 'positional goods,' politicians still believe that more top-down educational re-engineering is the way forward. Universities are being pushed into lowering standards for lower class entrants, and middle class parents are being deprived of the right to choose the schools their children attend, all in the name of achieving 'social justice'. These reports also seek to link the Old Labour project of income redistribution to the newer social mobility agenda by suggesting that income differences should be flattened to give people the opportunity to exploit their talents. But there is no evidence that lowering income inequality would stimulate mobility rather than discouraging it. The Milburn report also claims that, 'Unless child poverty is tackled, social mobility will be thwarted', but this is sheer hyperbole given that four out of five children growing up in 'poor' homes end up above the poverty line.

These four myths are pernicious in their effects, for the more often they are repeated, the more discouraged young people from humble social origins are likely to become. Tell somebody they are living in a country which respects hard work and rewards those who develop their talents to the full, and they will probably respond by strengthening their efforts in pursuit of success. Tell them that they are living in a 'closed shop society', and it would be no surprise if they just gave up and dropped out, thinking of themselves as victims of an unjust system.

The reality is that millions of men and women have worked their way up to responsible positions in British society having started life in relatively humble surroundings. Throughout business, the professions and the public services we find examples of individuals who have made good as a result of their own abilities and their own efforts. It would be helpful if our intellectuals and politicians could bring themselves to recognise and applaud this, rather than doing their best to deny it.

APPENDIX

Do We *Really* Want To Live in a Meritocracy?

The essence of a meritocratic society is that it offers individuals equal opportunities to become unequal. There is open competition for the most desirable, responsible and well-rewarded positions, and the most able and committed people generally succeed in attaining these positions.

It might be assumed that meritocracy is a 'good thing', both for the society (for it ensures that the most talented people get into the key leadership positions) and for individuals themselves (for it respects and justly rewards individual achievement). But a meritocracy can be an uncomfortable place in which to live, for it is inherently competitive, and it produces losers as well as winners. For this reason, the meritocratic ideal has many enemies, not least among egalitarians.

Meritocracy and social cohesion

In his introduction to his 2009 report on mobility in the professions, Alan Milburn suggests: 'Our society will not flourish unless people feel that effort and endeavour are rewarded.'[1] Similarly, in her introduction to the National Equality panel report of 2010, Harriet Harman writes: 'An equal society is more cohesive and at ease with itself. We are determined to tackle the unfairness that holds people back and give everyone the opportunity to succeed—make sure everyone has a fair chance.'[2]

This idea that meritocracy contributes to social cohesion can be traced back to the work of the late nineteenth century French sociologist, Emile Durkheim. He suggested that the intense social differentiation that is created by the complex division of labour in modern societies can be a source of strength, not (as many other commentators believed) a weakness.[3] Because everybody is different, we must all rely on each other, and our recognition of our mutual interdependence binds us together. However, for successful integration to occur, Durkheim insisted that individuals must be able to gravitate to the positions in society for which they are best suited. In his terminology, it was essential that the social division of labour should be 'spontaneous' rather than 'forced'.

Durkheim believed that individuals would never be happy (and modern societies would therefore never function properly) if they were obliged to perform functions in the social division of labour which were inappropriate to their talents and potentials: 'For the division of labour to produce solidarity, it is not sufficient that each have his task; it is still necessary that this task be fitting to him... If the institution of classes or castes sometimes gives rise to anxiety and pain instead of producing solidarity, this is because the distribution of social functions on which it rests does not respond, or rather no longer responds, to the distribution of natural talents... The division of labour produces solidarity only if it is spontaneous and in proportion as it is spontaneous... In short, *labour is divided spontaneously only if society is constituted in such a way that social inequalities exactly express natural inequalities.*'[4]

Note that Durkheim did not believe that inequality in itself is a problem. The problem only arises when individuals are prevented from gaining access to the social positions for which their talents have equipped them. As Durkheim put it, social inequalities must reflect 'natural inequalities'.

Durkheim was an advocate of both the 'weak' and the 'strong' versions of meritocratic policies identified in Chapter VII. Establishing true equality of opportunity would in his view entail abolishing privileges at the top (such as the right to inherit property) as well as extending opportunities at the bottom (e.g. by expanding access to education). This would allow individuals to distribute themselves between different social class positions in each generation on the basis of their natural talents, following which there would no longer be any grounds for envy, bitterness or anger.

Durkheim's belief that class inequalities need not generate class antagonisms provided recruitment is open and the competition is fair was further elaborated by sociologists in the USA in the 1950s who developed what they called a *functional theory of stratification*. Following Talcott Parsons, who saw that social stratification might contribute to social integration rather than tearing a society asunder, theorists like Kingsley Davis and Wilbert Moore proposed that societies need to recruit the most talented and able individuals to fill the most important positions, and that the only way of achieving this short of physical coercion is by means of some system of social inequality. They sought to demonstrate that the social positions of greatest functional importance (judged in terms of the number of other positions which depend upon them) tend in modern societies to be the most highly rewarded, and that a system of unequal financial rewards is necessary to encourage the most talented individuals to undergo the sacrifice of long-term training required by positions of high responsibility.[5] Like Durkheim, the functionalist theorists of the 1950s believed that social stratification could represent part of the solution to the problem of social cohesion, rather than (as in Marx's theory) part of the cause. For this to happen, however, it was necessary that talent be recognised and rewarded appropriately.

But how plausible is all this? Is meritocracy consistent with, even necessary for, social cohesion in modern societies? There is an opposite view which suggests that a meritocratic society will end up tearing itself apart.

Meritocracy and the emergence of 'cognitive stratification'

Michael Young, the sociologist who first coined the term 'meritocracy' in the 1950s, provides a clear and provocative statement of this second position. In *The Rise of the Meritocracy*, published in 1958, he developed a futuristic fable (a sort of 'social science fiction') purporting to be a social history of Britain written in the year 2034. His story tells of how an increasing premium had come to be placed on talent such that, by 1990, all individuals with high IQs were being recruited into the leading positions in society irrespective of their social backgrounds. This meant that the lower social strata were progressively stripped of their 'natural leaders' as talented individuals were selected out. Far from fostering social cohesion, as Durkheim would have predicted, this generated a festering resentment at the base of the society, for those individuals who remained in the lower strata were left to contemplate their own personal failure and could find nobody to blame but themselves. Residualised and marginalised by the stigma of failure, they were gradually attracted to a new form of radical populism aimed at replacing elitism based on intelligence with an egalitarian, classless society in which every individual was held in equal social esteem. Young's fable ends in the year 2033 when the Meritocracy was overthrown by a Populist revolt.

126

Young intended this story as a warning, for he believed that the meritocracy which he saw evolving in post-war Britain 'would be a more wounding, stratified system perhaps than had been known since the days of slavery'.[6] His worries have gained some credence from evidence gathered in the USA by Richard Herrnstein and Charles Murray in their controversial book, *The Bell Curve*. As we saw in chapter IV, this book attracted most attention for its claim that race and intelligence are related, but the core thesis of the book did not revolve around the issue of race. It was rather that meritocracy in the United States is generating a system of social stratification based upon 'cognitive classes', and that this threatens to undermine social cohesion.

Herrnstein and Murray based their analysis on two key propositions. First, class recruitment in the United States became more open during the course of the twentieth century, and for the first time in its history, the most intelligent individuals are now being selected for elite membership irrespective of their social origins. The change came about mainly through the expansion of higher education with college access now determined solely on the basis of ability. Secondly, the development of a high technology, knowledge-based society has meant that the number of jobs requiring high levels of intelligence and training has expanded, and that the market value of high intelligence has been rising. This means that the talented individuals from different social origins who get recruited into the 'cognitive elite' have been growing increasingly affluent.

As the brightest individuals are sucked out of the lower social strata, they come to form a relatively exclusive stratum based on membership of about a dozen main professions plus senior business executive positions. These people interact professionally and socially more or less exclusively with each other and have little realistic understanding of what is going on elsewhere in the society. Meanwhile, at the opposite end of the spectrum, those of low intelligence are left in an increasingly homogenous lower class, and the least intelligent gravitate towards a burgeoning underclass which contributes to many linked social problems (a large part of the book is devoted to demonstrating that it is low intelligence more than low social position which tends to generate poverty, crime, unemployment, welfare dependency, illegitimacy and political passivity). In parts of the inner cities, this has already led effectively to a 'fundamental breakdown in social organization' [7] which has prompted the high intelligence elite to flee from the state schools and the urban centres and to seek security in new gated communities.

The most likely outcome of all of this, according to the authors, is the strengthening of a 'custodial state' designed to maintain order through intensified intervention and surveillance while leaving the 'cognitive elite' free to go about its business. In short, meritocracy is producing the kind of social fragmentation and polarisation that Young was concerned about.

Herrnstein and Murray, and Young, were pointing in their different ways to a problem which Durkheim and the functionalist sociologists of the 1950s completely overlooked. Meritocracy might work for those who have 'merit', but it seems to offer little to those who do not. Why should those at the bottom, those who fail, accept the results of meritocratic selection as binding upon them? Why should they accept that their intellectual 'superior' should become their economic, social and political superiors?

Meritocracy and its discontents

This question raises two related issues associated with the growth of meritocracy. First, how can a meritocracy secure legitimacy in the eyes of those who fail (the problem of legitimation)? Second, how can it meet the expectations of those who succeed (the problem of 'positional goods' and coping with 'the revolution of expectations')? As society becomes more genuinely open, more genuinely meritocratic, so these two issues are likely to become ever more acute.

The problem of *legitimation* turns on the question of effective socialisation. If social position is determined at birth (as in a caste system), it is possible to prepare each generation for its fate. No false hopes are raised, no possibility of improving one's situation can be entertained. If social position is determined by a long-running talent contest, however, each generation spends its formative years anticipating the possibility of success, and the problem then arises of how to placate the eventual losers. Given that a meritocracy must be an open system, there is always likely to be a problem in inducing the eventual losers to accept their fate.

In an influential paper published in 1960, before the English grammar school system was all but abolished, Ralph Turner pinpointed the different ways in which the American and British education systems at that time sorted out children for eventual occupational placement.[8] He recognised that extensive social mobility could occur within both systems, but the way in which it occurred was different. In the American 'contest' system, many individuals competed for a limited number of prizes, and the contest was deemed to have been fair only if everybody was kept in the race right up to the bitter end so that their chance of winning was never taken away from them before the final result was declared. In the British 'sponsorship' system, by contrast, those individuals deemed to have the appropriate qualities were selected early for success (by means of the 11+ examination) and both the successful and unsuccessful were then put through training and socialisation appropriate to their future positions.

What is important about Turner's paper is his identification of the fundamental problem faced by a contest system, namely, how to 'cool out' the losers. He showed that American High School students often had hugely unrealistic expectations of their future career opportunities whereas the equivalent pupils in the British system were much more realistic. In Britain, realism bit harshly at age 11, but in the United States, realism dawned slowly, often as late as the college years. A contest ideology, in short, is likely to breed major disappointment and resentment.

Fifty years after Turner wrote that essay, British schooling has evolved into an American-style contest system. Selective schooling has virtually disappeared, and higher education has been opened up as a mass system, increasingly like that in America. This means that we now delay selection until age 16, and increasingly until age 21 (there is evidence that many employers are now recruiting graduates only from a select range of universities, for example). The result is that, as we have tried to extend the field of opportunity, so we have ended up making eventual failure that much more difficult to bear.[9]

This brings us to the second issue, the problem of *positional goods.* The problem here is that, the more people who are enabled to succeed, the less value attaches to success and the more severe are the penalties of failure. We saw in Chapter VII that higher education is a classic 'positional good', for the more people who have it, the less valuable it becomes as a means of entering top positions, and the greater is the penalty for those who fail to get access to it at all. But as the middle class got larger over the last hundred years, the same argument has come to apply to upward social mobility itself.

When most of the society is working class, it is a huge bonus to achieve upward mobility into the middle class, but when such movement becomes common, the advantages decline. The more the opportunities for social mobility have opened up, the less they seem to offer. In such a situation, it is easy to see how a more open and fluid society may become a less cohesive and contented one.

There is a long history of sociological research which demonstrates that the most acute resentment is often felt in situations of widening opportunity. In his classic review of Stouffer's research on promotion prospects in the American military, for example, Robert Merton noted that those units with the highest promotion rates recorded the lowest levels of satisfaction, and vice versa. He showed this was because high rates of promotion encouraged those in the ranks to compare themselves with those who had been elevated with the result that they felt aggrieved at being passed over. Low promotion rates, on the other hand, encouraged identification with others remaining in the same position as oneself, and therefore fostered greater contentment.[10]

The implications of this for an open, dynamic society are obvious. With limited rates of social mobility, nobody expects to move up, and everybody is fairly contented with their lot. With extensive social mobility, many people move up, and those who are left behind begin to compare their situation unfavourably with that of their more successful peers. It is in this sense that a move to greater meritocracy is likely to generate increased frustration and resentment in society.

It seems from this that the pursuit of meritocracy can be almost self-defeating. The more opportunities are held open for people, the more difficult it is for those who fail to accept the result as legitimate, the less likely it is that those who succeed will feel any great sense of benefit, and the more resentful people are likely to become when they fail to emulate the success of their neighbours. These problems do not necessarily threaten social breakdown and fragmentation, but they can generate widespread disillusionment among successes and failures alike.

Alternatives to meritocracy

If meritocracy turns out to be so problematic, what are the alternatives? There are two major contenders: egalitarianism and libertarianism.

The *egalitarian* case against meritocracy is that it is morally wrong to reward people on the basis of their talents (and, perhaps, also their effort). Where meritocracy requires only equality of opportunity as the criterion of 'social justice', egalitarianism requires equality of outcomes ('end-state' equality).

There are two versions of this argument. The first is already familiar from Chapter IV. It holds that there are no innate differences of ability between people and that talent, like effort, is merely the product of a privileged environment. Rewarding ability is thus tantamount to rewarding the children of the more privileged classes, which means that meritocracy turns out to be just another way in which dominant classes try to justify their continuing hold on top positions in society.

As we saw in chapter IV, many sociologists have adopted this line of attack, and it is one which remains common within so-called 'progressive' circles to this day.[11] Egalitarians dislike the idea of selection and competition and they would prefer a situation where there are no losers. They particularly dislike meritocratic selection because it seems to justify inequalities which they would prefer did not exist. As Daniel Bell has shown, this leads them to attack the very idea that there are any natural differences of ability between people, for to undermine the concept of intelligence is to undermine the very basis of meritocratic selection. If there are no natural differences between people, and if differences of ability arise simply out of unearned privilege, then it follows that nobody merits anything more than anybody else. In this way, the ideal of equality of opportunity is replaced by the much more radical ideal of equalising outcomes. [12]

This kind of argument is clearly vulnerable to the growing weight of evidence that there *are* natural differences between people, and this has given rise to the second variant of the egalitarian critique of meritocracy. This grudgingly accepts that there may be some innate differences between people, but denies that this is any reason to reward them differently. This is a much more challenging version of the argument, for it poses the pertinent question of why individuals should expect to be rewarded for talents which they were lucky enough to be born with and which they have themselves done nothing to deserve.

This is the position adopted by A.H. Halsey, John Goldthorpe's principal collaborator on the Nuffield College social mobility project. He explicitly denies that what he calls the 'liberal principle of "justice as desert"' should be accepted as the criterion of social fairness.[13] The argument was later reiterated by Gordon Marshall and Adam Swift in a critique of my work on social mobility: 'It [is] particularly apt to ask whether an inherited characteristic—genetically-determined intelligence —is an appropriate basis for reward at all. A crucial issue here would seem to be the distinction between those attributes for which the individual can claim responsibility and those which are his or hers merely by chance. If someone possesses particular talents or skills merely as a result of the natural lottery then it is not clear how justice is served by rewarding such possession.'[14]

Implicit in this argument is an appeal to a conception of social justice associated with the work of John Rawls.[15] Rawls suggested that we should gauge social justice with reference to the social arrangements which individuals would agree upon were they all in an 'original position' in which none of them knew what their personal attributes would be and all were ignorant of the place which they would occupy in society. Operating behind such a 'veil of ignorance', Rawls argued persuasively that we would all agree that resources should be shared out equally, except in those situations where an unequal distribution could be shown to produce greater benefits for those who are least well off than they could possibly enjoy under any other social arrangement (what he called the 'difference principle').

Rawlsian logic suggests that meritocracy is inconsistent with social justice. In the original position, we would not choose to be born into a meritocracy because none of us could be sure whether we would be born bright or dull, and none of us would know whether we would be hard working or lazy by character. Furthermore, meritocracy violates the difference principle (e.g. by offering more training to brighter people). The safest option for those in the original position would be to reject meritocracy and go for end-state equality (the egalitarian ideal).

The problem with this reasoning, however, is that in reality, we *do* know what abilities we have to offer, and we *do* know whether we are inclined to shirk or work hard (indeed, we can also do something to change these things by our own efforts). We know our potential and our inclination to use it, because these things are central to our characters and personalities—to what it is that makes us each a distinctive human being. To ignore them, as Rawls seeks to do in setting up his original position, is to treat us merely as clones of one another and to deny to us any responsibility for what happens in our lives.

Rawls arrives at the conclusion that the particular attributes of individual persons should be treated as the common property of the entire society. He does not go so far as to suggest eradicating all natural differences, but this is only because he wants to harness people's talents to the treadmill of the common good. He insists that, because talented individuals do not deserve their talent, it must be seen as a collective resource which must be devoted, not to the pursuit of individual gain or pleasure, but to furthering the interests of those who are least well off.

Robert Nozick has developed a thorough-going critique of this whole approach.[16] He accepts that, viewed from the original position, social inequalities deriving from differences of natural ability would never be viewed as just, but he says that by setting up the question of social justice as one to be resolved by people in the original position, Rawls has rigged the game. Only one result is possible—an agreement on end state equality—because all the information relevant to making a sensible judgement is denied to us. But why deny us this information?

In the real world, success is not a natural resource waiting to be shared out. Success is achieved by individuals (often talented and hard working individuals) who, in the process, establish an entitlement to its rewards. Nozick gives the example of students taking an examination. Put into a Rawlsian original position and asked how the grades should be distributed, they would have little option but to agree on an equal share out. In reality, however, they would never agree to such an arrangement, for some of them have revised hard with the aim of getting good grades while others have spent every night in the bar. An equal share-out of grades would be seen by many of them as grossly unjust, and those who favoured it would more likely be motivated by envy or avarice than by any genuine desire to see justice done.

There is, in other words, an entitlement to reward which Rawls's approach deliberately suppresses. Why should those who have created their own rewards be expected to give them up to those who have made no effort? What kind of principle of justice is it that seeks to make the talented and the motivated work for the least well off members of their community without even asking why it is that the least well-off have so little as compared with them?

Nozick's critique of Rawls rescues the principle of meritocracy from the egalitarian attack. Following Nozick, the answer to the question posed by Marshall and Swift—why should we treat talent as deserving of reward?—is that talented members of a meritocracy deserve their rewards *if they have established an entitlement to them through their own efforts*. If (as in the parable of the three talents), people with ability do not use it, then they establish no entitlement. It is not ability *per se* which is rewarded in a meritocracy; it is ability put to good effect. We do not select bright people into good jobs and pay them well simply as a reward for being bright. We do it (or, rather, employers and consumers of goods and services do it) because bright people *use* their ability in such a way that others are willing to transfer entitlements to them.

This reasoning underpins the *libertarian* conception of fairness based in a theory of just entitlement. Nozick argues that rewards follow entitlement and that entitlement can be established through three principles: just acquisition (established by producing resources oneself or through the freely contracted help of others), just transfer (through voluntary gifts or exchange), and rectification of past injustices (i.e. reallocation of resources in those cases where either of the first two principles has been violated). Put into practice, this means that individuals have a right to the money they have earned and to the money which others have freely given them.

Nozick's theory seems to pose a problem for the meritocracy ideal, however, for it is a theory of entitlement, not a theory of just deserts. It has nothing to say about rewarding talent or effort as such. It will often be the case that talented and hard working people end up establishing entitlement to substantial rewards, but this does not always happen. Lazy people with little ability might also end up rich or successful— they might simply find themselves in the right place at the right time, or they might inherit a company from their parents, or they might scoop the jackpot on the national lottery. Luck, caprice, fluke, effort, all are equally legitimate as a basis for reward provided they involve no direct coercion of other people. The question of whether people deserve their good fortune is, for Nozick, irrelevant.

We find the same problem in the work of Friedrich Hayek. With disarming frankness, Hayek accepts that market capitalism can some-times reward those whom we tend to think of as undeserving while meting out harsh treatment to those who display genuine merit. The talented individual who works hard but fails to find a market for his or her services will fail, just as the rogue who manages to convince others that they want what he or she is offering will succeed. For Hayek, there is nothing 'wrong' with this, and there is nothing to be done to rectify it. He assures us that in a free society, it will normally be the case that rewards flow to those individuals who put their talents to good use in providing a genuine service of value to other people, but he resists the idea that such an outcome should be engineered or enforced simply because we think of it as desirable: 'However able a man may be in a particular field, the value of his services is necessarily low in a free society unless he also possesses the capacity of making his ability known to those who can derive the greatest benefit from it. Though it may offend our sense of justice to find that of two men who by equal effort have acquired the same specialized skill and knowledge, one may be a success and the other a failure, we must recognize that in a free society it is the use of particular opportunities that determines usefulness... In a free society we are remunerated not for our skill but for using it rightly.'[17]

Hayek is, of course, critical of the egalitarian position, arguing that the inherent differences between individuals mean that end-state equality could only be achieved by treating them unequally (i.e. unfairly). But in the end, he is just as critical of the meritocratic position, arguing (like Marshall and Swift) that there is no credit to be claimed for talents which one happens to have acquired by accident of genetics, and that a meritocratic society would undermine liberty if it tried to fix rewards according to people's attributes rather than according to their entitlements. For Hayek, as for Nozick, all that matters is that we should come by our success without coercing others, not that we should 'deserve' it.

It seems that having saved the meritocratic ideal from the egalitarian critique, we have ended up losing it again through a retreat into libertarianism. Neither egalitarians nor libertarians have any reason to be particularly interested in the kind of analysis of social mobility developed in this book, for neither sees any good reason why we should be concerned about rewarding talent and hard work:

- For egalitarians, what matters is that people should get the same at the end of the day, so if I end up in a low-paid, low status job because I have no aptitude for anything better, and you end up in a well-paid high status job because you work every hour of the day and pursue your ambition to its limits, the results are deemed unjust because they are unequal.

- For libertarians, what matters is that people should be able to keep whatever they happen to have freely acquired, so if I have no talent but am given a good job because my brother is on the Board, and if you are bright and committed but are denied an appointment because my brother happens to dislike the look of your face, no injustice has been done.

Starting from opposite extremes, these two critiques of meritocracy meet, absurdly, in the middle.

We are all meritocrats now

Against both of these positions, the underlying premise of this book has been that it *does* matter why people end up in the positions they do. Both the egalitarian and libertarian positions have some intuitive sense to them, but in the end, they both founder on the fact that, in a modern society like contemporary Britain, there is a strong and shared sense of fairness and justice which demands that there be some link between individual talent and effort on the one hand, and reward through occupational success on the other. As Geoff Dench has suggested, 'The basic idea of meritocracy is rooted in principles of exchange and reciprocity that lie at the heart of all social systems, and that enjoy high levels of acceptance in all cultures.'[18]

Consistently with the egalitarian position, most of us do feel some sympathy for those who fail, but we also generally demand to know whether this has followed from their own stupidity or recklessness or was a result of circumstances largely beyond their control. This is why the social welfare system for so many centuries attempted to distinguish the 'deserving' poor from the 'undeserving' and to treat them differently, and it is why so many people today feel angry at the thought that their hard work and personal effort is being taxed in order to support those who will not work in addition to those who cannot.[19] Popular support for egalitarianism is always qualified by the question of just desert.

The same is true of support for libertarianism. Consistently with the libertarian position, few of us feel genuinely aggrieved by those who make good simply because they are 'lucky'. National lottery jackpot winners are not widely resented for their good fortune, and although we may feel some envy when we hear of somebody who has come into an inheritance or has stumbled upon a new invention which makes them a millionaire, most of us simply shrug, smile, and mutter 'Good luck to them!' We do, however, resent those who get to positions of wealth and influence through nepotism or the mobilisation of privileged social networks rather than through open competition, and we get justifiably angry about the allocation of positions on the basis of ascribed rather than achieved characteristics (e.g. allocation of jobs by race or gender rather than by talent or effort is widely held to be offensive).

Why are we generally happy to help out people who fall on hard times but not those who are feckless? Why are we happy to let lucky people enjoy their good fortune but not those who have gained success by virtue of their family connections? The common factor in all of this is the belief that we should all be treated according to the same criteria. If I have to work in order to gain a living, then others who are also capable of working should not expect to live off my earnings. If I have to compete on the basis of my talent and effort in order to get a good job, then others should not be able to walk into top positions simply because they play golf with the boss's son. The lottery winner does not offend us because the rules are clear and we can all buy a ticket, and the beneficiary of a will does not offend us because we all enjoy the right to use our own money as we see fit, including giving it to others. It is when the rules are bent to favour one party over another that the collective sense of justice gets badly bruised.

Nozick and Hayek seek to reassure us that success normally coincides with merit (because, in a free market, rational buyers, including employers of labour, will choose the best services or products irrespective of the race, gender or social connections of those supplying them), but they accept that there is no necessary connection between the two, and they see no reason for government to step in to try to prevent 'irrational' discrimination against those with merit. Yet as Nozick himself recognises, 'People will not long accept a distribution they believe is *unjust*. People want their society to be and to look just.'[20]

This means that rules have to be established which ensure, as far as possible, that the competition which we are all entering is a fair one.

There is, in the end, something unsatisfactory about a libertarian ethic which allows the 'deserving' to be disadvantaged without trying to do anything about it, just as there is something unsatisfactory about an egalitarian ethic which allows the 'undeserving' to be advantaged without trying to prevent it. Libertarians *do* have a problem in justifying caprice or bigotry as the basis for rewarding one individual while denying another, just as egalitarians *do* have a problem in justifying laziness or stupidity as legitimate grounds for doling out resources which other people have earned. Because both positions refuse to be drawn on the issue of merit, neither finally satisfies that generalised sense of fair competition on which the legitimacy of modern capitalist societies ultimately depends.

Back in the 1990s, I organised a survey in which a sample of the British population was asked to respond to three different statements about the 'fairest' way to establish individual entitlement to material resources:[21]

- One of these statements represented the egalitarian ideal that 'people's incomes should be made more equal by taxing higher earners'. Just over half of the sample agreed with this while around one-third disagreed.

- A second statement expressed the free market, libertarian position that 'people's incomes should depend on market demand for their services'. Again, something more than a half of respondents agreed and around one-third disagreed.

- The final statement reflected the meritocratic ideal that 'people's incomes should depend on hard work and ability'. Fully 90 per cent of respondents agreed with this with fewer than 10 per cent disagreeing.

Few moral principles can command universal assent in a modern, pluralistic, individualistic society, but meritocracy clearly comes pretty close.[22]

This strong support for meritocracy relative to the other two positions suggests that most of us understand that inequality is not in itself 'unfair'—it depends on whether it results from the application of individual talent and effort. If we are convinced that, by and large, those who have the ability and who make an effort can usually gain success, then the basis is laid for a society which can function reasonably harmoniously. Meritocracy does have a problem dealing with the social consequences of failure, but this need not undermine social cohesion provided the competition is known to have been fair. Ninety per cent agreement is not a bad basis on which to build and sustain a moral social order.

This is why the research findings outlined in this book are so important, for they give the lie to those who seek to convince us that meritocracy in Britain is a sham. I suspect that many of the social pathologies which have escalated over the last 50 years in Britain—the criminality and anti-social behaviour, the denial of personal responsibility, the mindless pursuit of hedonism, the readiness to accept dependency on others—have something to do with the spread of an egalitarian ideology which insists that social selection is rigged and that the dice are loaded. If people born into relatively disadvantaged circumstances are repeatedly told that the competition has been fixed so they cannot win, then of course they will conclude that it makes no sense for them to join the game. State dependency or criminality are then the only other games they can join.

We have seen that occupational selection, by and large, is not rigged. The dice are not heavily loaded. The competition has not been fixed in advance. The game is worth playing, even for those born into the poorest social conditions. But many of our politicians and intellectual leaders seem not to believe this. Rather than instilling hope and aspiration in our young people, they peddle a gloomy ideology of defeatism and victimhood which in the end can only undermine the motivation and self-confidence of those they say they want to help. We live in an open society where talent and motivation are the key drivers of success and achievement. The most positive contribution politicians could make would be to acknowledge and celebrate this fact rather than seeking to deny it.

Notes

Introduction

1   Peter Bauer, *Equality, the Third World and Economic Delusion*, London: Weidenfeld & Nicolson, 1981, chapter 2.

2   Peter Saunders, *Unequal But Fair? A Study of class barriers in Britain*, London: Institute of Economic Affairs, Health & Welfare Unit, 1996.

3   See Geoff Dench's interview with Michael Young, 'Looking back on *Meritocracy*' in Geoff Dench (ed.), *The Rise and Rise of Meritocracy*, Blackwell Publishing, 2006.

4   Michael Young, *The Rise of the Meritocracy*, London: Thames and Hudson, 1958, p. 94.

5   A.H. Halsey, *A History of Sociology in Britain*, Oxford University Press 2004, Tables 8.5 and 8.6. Not surprisingly, Halsey concludes, 'The sociology profession has become politicized', p. 162.

6   For an explanation of how 'dominant paradigms' guide 'normal science', see Alan Buckingham and Peter Saunders, *The Survey Methods Workbook* Cambridge: Polity Press, 2004, chapter 1.

7   Classes may be identified in various ways, but the aim is to group people together who share common economic situations. This involves more than just similar incomes, for members of the same class tend to enjoy similar levels of prosperity, economic security, health and wellbeing as well. See Anthony Heath and Clive Payne, 'Twentieth Century Trends in Social Mobility in Britain' Centre for Research into Elections and Social Trends, *Working Paper* no. 70, June 1999, University of Oxford, p. 2.

8   'All cited in Peter Wilby, 'A delay on the road to meritocracy', in Geoff Dench (ed.), *The Rise and Rise of Meritocracy*, pp. 215-16. In his introduction to this volume, Dench himself makes the point that New Labour's embrace of meritocracy appears almost dismissive of its traditional working class, manual worker constituency. The emphasis is on the importance of acquiring formal qualifications, and this reflects the values of a public sector ruling elite which has little regard for other forms of employment. Wilby hints at the same thing when he notes of Blair's 2001 speech that, almost as an afterthought, he added: 'Of course we should value all our citizens, not just those who rise to the top' (p. 216).

9   Cabinet Office Strategy Unit, *Getting On, Getting Ahead*, November 2008.

10 *Unleashing Aspiration: The final report of the panel on fair access to the professions* (the Milburn Report), 2009.

11 John Hills and others, *An Anatomy of Economic Inequality in the UK*, London: Government Equalities Office, 2010.

12   *Unleashing Aspiration*, p. 6.

13   The Conservative Party report, *Through the Glass Ceiling: A Conservative Agenda for Social Mobility* begins with the words: 'Britain is no longer a socially mobile nation. We fall far behind many of our international competitors in offering people a route up the social ladder, even though past generations in this country did have such route' (p. 2).

14   Chapters III, VI and VII are entirely new. Other chapters draw selectively on material included in the earlier book but also include new material published since 1996.

1: Absolute Mobility: How Tall are the Ladders; How Long are the Snakes?

1   'The Labour cabinet includes the Miliband brothers, Edward and David; the husband-and-wife team, Ed Balls and Yvette Cooper; Harriet Harman, the niece of Lord Longford (a former Labour leader of the House of Lords) and the spouse of the party's treasurer, Jack Dromey; Douglas Alexander, sibling of Wendy, the former leader of Labour in Scotland; Hillary Benn, son of Tony, who served as Harold Wilson's industry secretary and Jim Callaghan's energy secretary; and Peter Mandelson, grandson of Herbert Morrison, Clement Attlee's deputy prime minister. All of which presents an awkward challenge to a report on social mobility from Alan Milburn which insists, "Background and social network should not be the critical factors in determining or allocating opportunities"', (Jeff Randall, 'How the class war backfired and put social mobility into retreat', *Daily Telegraph*, 31 July 2009).

2   It is, however, worth noting that, even among the elite, meritocratic recruitment is by no means as rare as is often assumed. Anthony Heath, *Social Mobility*, London: Fontana, 1981, reports that in the 1970s, 11 per cent of top civil servants, 19 per cent of Church of England bishops, 27 per cent of ambassadors, 28 per cent of High Court judges, and 45 per cent of bank directors had been born to parents occupying elite positions. Even at these rarified heights, therefore, recruitment from outside the elite clearly predominates over elite self-recruitment. Moreover, many of the richest individuals in Britain have accumulated their wealth through their own efforts rather than through accident of birth. The annual *Sunday Times* reviews of the richest thousand people in the country consistently reveal many more 'self-made' men and women than inheritors. In the 2004 report, for example, only 249 of the richest thousand had inherited their wealth, while the rest had accumulated it themselves (this represented a marked shift from 1991 when half were inheritors). See Richard Beresford and Stephen Boyd, *The Sunday Times Rich List* 18 April 2004.

3   Quoted in John Goldthorpe, *Social Mobility and Class Structure in Modern Britain*, second edn, Oxford: Clarendon Press, 1987, p. 21.

4   Tom Bottomore, *Classes in Modern Society*, London: George Allen & Unwin, 1965, pp. 16, 38, 40.

5   Ralph Miliband, *The State in Capitalist Society*, London: Weidenfeld & Nicolson, 1969, pp. 41-42. Professor Miliband was the father of the Miliband brothers who now sit in the Labour cabinet.

6   Peter Worsley, *Introducing Sociology*, Harmondsworth: Penguin, 1970, pp. 298, 301.

7   Anthony Giddens, *The Class Structure of the Advanced Societies*, London: Hutchinson, 1973, pp. 181-82.

8   John Westergaard and Henrietta Resler, *Class in a Capitalist Society*, London: Heinemann, 1975, pp. 299, 302, 312.

9   David Glass, *Social Mobility in Britain*, London: Routledge & Kegan Paul, 1954.

10   Such claims continued to be taught well into the 1990s. In 1992, for example, Professor Richard Scase published a student text in which he authoritatively asserted: 'There is a high degree of intergenerational inheritance of managerial and professional jobs on the one hand, and of manual occupations on the other. If there is any intergenerational openness it is among lower grade technical, lesser professional and routine non-manual occupations' (*Class*, Open University Press, 1992, p. 53). This claim simply cannot be reconciled with evidence available to sociologists since 1980 showing that 22 per cent of children of working class origins get to the professional-managerial class, and that 38 per cent of children born into the professional-managerial class fail to stay there.

11   Geoff Payne, *Mobility and Change in Modern Society*, Basingstoke: MacMillan, 1987.

12   Payne, *Mobility and Change in Modern Society*, p. 89.

13   Gordon Marshall, Howard Newby, David Rose and Carolyn Vogler, *Social Class in Modern Britain*, London: Hutchinson, 1988.

14   Payne, *Mobility and Change in Modern Society*.

15   Anthony Heath and Clive Payne, 'Twentieth Century Trends in Social Mobility in Britain' Centre for Research into Elections and Social Trends, *Working Paper* No. 70, June 1999, University of Oxford. Heath and Payne use Goldthorpe's schema and define 'upward mobility' as all movements into class I (the upper service class), out of class VII (semi- and unskilled manual workers) and upwards into class II (the lower service class). The analysis did not go beyond

those born in 1959 to ensure that everyone was old enough to reach career maturity (assumed to occur after the age of 35).

[16] By then, 9,175 of the original subjects were still in the survey. For details go to the Centre for Longitudinal Studies web site; http://www.cls.ioe.ac.uk/text.asp?section=000100020003

[17] http://www.cls.ioe.ac.uk/studies.asp?section=000100020002. In 2004, there were 9,316 of the original participants left in the sample.

[18] John Goldthorpe and Michelle Jackson, 'Intergenerational class mobility in contemporary Britain' *British Journal of Sociology*, vol. 58, 2007, pp. 525-46. This analysis uses the 7-class version of Goldthorpe's social class schema. Movement between classes III, IV (b and c) and V is defined as 'horizontal mobility' since these classes are not hierarchically ordered relative to each other.

[19] Data abstracted from Tables II and III in Goldthorpe and Jackson, 'Intergenerational class mobility in contemporary Britain' *op cit.* Service class defined as classes I, II and IVa (small proprietors with employees); working class defined as classes VI and VII.

[20] Trevor Noble reports that more than half of the total shift in class positions from one generation to the next takes place in the course of the second generation's own career—i.e. in between starting work and the eventual destination achieved. This suggests that, 'Purely intergenerational comparisons... tend to underplay the total experience of social mobility in the population as a whole' (Trevor Noble, 'The mobility transition: Social mobility trends in the first half of the 21st century', *Sociology*, vol. 34, 2000, p. 37).

[21] Noble, 'The mobility transition'.

[22] R. Erikson and J. Goldthorpe, *The Constant Flux: A Study of Class Mobility in Industrial Societies*, Oxford: Clarendon Press, 1992.

[23] Anna Cristina d'Addio, 'Intergenerational transmission of disadvantage' *Social, Employment and Migration Working Paper*, no. 52, Paris, OECD, 2007, p. 29

[24] Stephen Aldridge, *Social Mobility: A Discussion Paper*, Cabinet Office Performance & Innovation Unit, April 2001, para. 38.

[25] John Hills and others, *An Anatomy of Economic Inequality in the UK*, London: Government Equalities Office, 2010, chapter 11.

[26] Hills, *An Anatomy of Economic Inequality in the UK*, Fig.11.2.

[27] d'Addio, 'Intergenerational transmission of disadvantage'; Erikson and Goldthorpe, *The Constant Flux*; Richard Breen, *Social Mobility in Europe*, Oxford University Press, 2004.

[28] d'Addio, 'Intergenerational transmission of disadvantage'; David Goodhart, 'More mobile than we think' *Prospect*, 20 December 2008.

[29] Data from Hertz, reported in Table 2 of Jo Blanden, 'How much can we learn from international comparisons of intergenerational mobility?' London School of Economics Centre for Economics of Education *Departmental Paper* November 2009. Measured by a coefficient of association β, Britain ranks lower at 28th. This is because there is relatively little variance in parental years of schooling as compared with other countries, and the β is influenced by differences of variances while correlation coefficients are not.

[30] Jo Blanden, Paul Gregg, Stephen Machin, *Intergenerational mobility in Europe and North America*, Centre for Economic Performance, London School of Economics, April 2005.

[31] Jo Blanden, 'How much can we learn from international comparisons of intergenerational mobility?', p. 15.

[32] Blanden, 'How much can we learn from international comparisons of intergenerational mobility?', p. 15. Emphasis added.

[33] Hills, *An Anatomy of Economic Inequality in the UK*, p. 329.

2: Relative Mobility

[1] As Geoff Payne has argued in respect of Goldthorpe's emphasis on relative measures: 'It is essentially a pessimistic view which leads the reader towards seeing British society as more closed and thereby more *static* than is necessary... There is considerable fluidity; certainly sufficient fluidity to require of us as sociologists that we come to terms with it. Goldthorpe directs our attention away from it, in part because of the narrow view of his subject, derived from his political position, and part because he underestimates the significance of the key process in mobility, namely occupational transition... ' Geoff Payne, *Mobility and Change in Modern Society*, Basingstoke: MacMillan, 1987, p. 119.

[2] John Goldthorpe, *Social Mobility and Class Structure in Modern Britain*, second edn, Oxford: Clarendon Press, 1987, pp. 327, 328.

[3] The 1983 survey results are reported in the second edition of Goldthorpe's book, in chapter 9, which is co-authored with Clive Payne.

[4] Gordon Marshall, Howard Newby, David Rose and Carolyn Vogler, *Social Class in Modern Britain*, London, Hutchinson, 1988, p. 138.

[5] Anthony Heath and Clive Payne, 'Twentieth Century Trends in Social Mobility in Britain' Centre for Research into Elections and Social Trends, *Working Paper* no. 70, June 1999, University of Oxford.

[6] Richard Breen and John Goldthorpe, 'Class, mobility and merit' *European Sociological Review*, vol. 17, 2001, pp. 81-101.

[7] Peter Saunders, *Unequal But Fair? A Study of class barriers in Britain*, London: Institute of Economic Affairs, Health & Welfare Unit, 1996. The original data in Table 3 of the book referred to men and women together. The figures for men only have been substituted here to give comparability with the other sources. Similar calculations on the same data set are reported in Paul Johnson and Howard Reed, 'Two nations? The inheritance of poverty and affluence', Institute for Fiscal Studies *Commentary*, no. 53, 1996.

[8] Heath and Payne contrast Goldthorpe's classes I and II with his classes V, VI and VII, although Goldthorpe himself treats class V (lower grade technicians and supervisors) as one of the 'intermediate classes.' The data from Breen and Goldthorpe exclude class V from the 'working class', while my analysis used Office of Population Censuses and Surveys (OPCS) class categories rather than the Goldthorpe schema. I contrast OPCS classes I and II with OPCS classes IV and V. Elsewhere (Peter Saunders, 'Reflections on the meritocracy debate in Britain', *British Journal of Sociology*, vol. 53, 2002, pp. 559-574) I have shown that this division correlates closely with Goldthorpe's service class/working class division (84 per cent of those in Goldthorpe's service class were coded to Registrar General classes I/II in my analysis, and 98 per cent of those in Goldthorpe's bottom class were coded to Registrar General class IV/V in my analysis).

[9] Adam Swift, 'Class analysis from a normative perspective' *British Journal of Sociology*, vol. 51, 2000, p. 665.

[10] See, for example, Goldthorpe, *Social Mobility and Class Structure in Modern Britain,* p. 328.

[11] Goldthorpe, *Social Mobility and Class Structure in Modern Britain,* p. 114.

[12] Heath and Payne, 'Twentieth Century Trends in Social Mobility in Britain', p. 24.

[13] Trevor Noble, 'Occupational mobility and social change in Britain', *Hitotsubashi Journal of Social Studies*, vol. 27, 1995, pp. 65-90. See also Trevor Noble, *Unexamined assumptions and neglected questions in social mobility research* Unpublished paper, Dept of Sociology, University of Sheffield, 2001

[14] Trevor Noble, 'The mobility transition: Social mobility trends in the first half of the 21st century', *Sociology*, vol. 34, 2000, p. 36

[15] Richard Breen, and John Goldthorpe, 'Class inequality and meritocracy: A critique of Saunders and an alternative analysis,' *British Journal of Sociology*, 1999, vol. 50, p. 5.

[16] Breen, and Goldthorpe, 'Class inequality and meritocracy', fn.3.

[17] John Goldthorpe and Michelle Jackson, 'Intergenerational class mobility in contemporary Britain' *British Journal of Sociology*, vol. 58, 2007, pp. 525-46, Table VII.

[18] R. Erikson and J. Goldthorpe, The Constant Flux: A Study of Class Mobility in Industrial Societies, Oxford: Clarendon Press, 1992.

[19] Jonathon Gershuny, 'Beating the odds (1): Inter-generational social mobility from a human capital perspective' University of Essex, Institute for Social & Economic Research *Working papers* no.17, 2002.

[20] Paul Lambert, Ken Prandy and Wendy Bottero, 'By slow degrees: Two centuries of social reproduction and mobility in Britain' *Sociological research Online,* vol. 12, 2007, para 5.1; http://www.socresonline.org.uk/12/1/prandy.html

3: Is Social Mobility Falling?

[1] This is particularly true of middle class people who typically start off with relatively low earnings and become much better paid as their careers develop. The age at which income is assessed will in this case make a big difference to how it is estimated. To overcome this problem, economists sometimes adjust parental income data to take account of other variables like occupation and education, but this obviously opens up further possibilities for error.

[2] The fact that mobility rates measured in this way are inherently relative can create problems when comparing mobility rates across countries, for movements between quartiles can mean very different things in different countries in terms of absolute income shifts, depending on the dispersal and skew of their income distributions.

[3] Paul Johnson and Howard Reed, 'Two nations? The inheritance of poverty and affluence' Institute for Fiscal Studies *Commentary* No.53, 1996, Table 15.

[4] L. Dearden, S. Machin and H. Reed, 'Intergenerational mobility in Britain' London School of Economics, Centre for Economic Performance *Discussion Paper*, no. 281, March 1996, p. 30.

[5] Jo Blanden, Paul Gregg & Stephen Machin, *Intergenerational mobility in Europe and North America* Centre for Economic Performance, London School of Economics, April 2005.

[6] Jo Blanden, Paul Gregg and Stephen Machin, 'Social mobility in Britain: Low and falling' *CentrePiece*, Spring 2005, pp. 18-20; Blanden, Gregg and Macmillan, 'Accounting for intergenerational income persistence' *The Economic Journal* vol.117, 2007, C45-C60; Blanden, Gregg and Macmillan, 'Intergenerational

persistence in income and social class' Centre for Market and Public Organisation *Working Paper* 08/195, University of Bristol, 2008; Blanden and Machin, 'Up and down the generational income ladder in Britain' *National Institute Economic Review*, No.205, 2008, pp. 101-116.

[7]   Blanden, Gregg and Machin, *Intergenerational mobility in Europe and North America*, p. 8.

[8]   Again, we should note that both of these correlation coefficients indicate rather weak associations (as a rule of thumb, correlations below 0.3 are generally regarded as weak), confirming that inter-generational income mobility is extensive in both studies—although problems in measuring parental incomes accurately over an extended period may be deflating the size of the correlation coefficient.

[9]   David Blunkett, The Inclusive Society? Social Mobility in 21st century Britain London: Progress, January 2008, p. 10.

[10] Fernando Galindo-Rueda and Anna Vignoles, *Class-ridden or Meritocratic? An economic analysis of recent changes in Britain*, London School of Economics, Centre for Economics of Education, May 2003, p. 37.

[11] Blanden, Gregg and Macmillan, 'Accounting for intergenerational income persistence'.

[12] David Willetts, *The Pinch: How the Baby Boomers took their children's future—and why they should give it back*, Atlantic Books, 2010, p. 208.

[13] Stephen Machin and Anna Vignoles, 'Educational inequality: The widening socio-economic gap' *Fiscal Studies*, vol. 25, 2004, Table 2.

[14] Machin and Vignoles, 'Educational inequality', p. 119.

[15] Blanden, Gregg and Macmillan, 'Accounting for intergenerational income persistence'.

[16] Blanden and Machin, 'Up and down the generational income ladder in Britain'.

[17] Blanden and Machin, 'Up and down the generational income ladder in Britain', p. 110.

[18] Cabinet Office Strategy Unit, *Getting On, Getting Ahead*, November 2008, pp. 3-4 and 6.

[19] Although the Cabinet Office report suggests both trends could be true if income inequalities have been increasing faster within social classes than between them —*Getting On, Getting Ahead*, p. 29.

[20] John Goldthorpe and Michelle Jackson, 'Intergenerational class mobility in contemporary Britain' *British Journal of Sociology*, vol. 58, 2007, pp. 525-46.

[21] Goldthorpe and Jackson, 'Intergenerational class mobility in contemporary Britain', p. 539.

[22] John Goldthorpe and Colin Mills, 'Trends in intergenerational class mobility in modern Britain', *National Institute Economic Review*, no. 205, 2008, pp. 83-100.

[23] Goldthorpe and Mills, 'Trends in intergenerational class mobility in modern Britain', pp. 94-5.

[24] Studies of class mobility commonly compare children's destinations with the class of their father. Where attempts are made to take account of a second parental occupation, it is usually done by classifying both parents according to the 'dominant' or higher class of the two—which is usually the father's.

[25] Blanden, Gregg and Macmillan, 'Accounting for intergenerational income persistence', p. C54.

[26] Blanden, Gregg and Macmillan, 'Intergenerational persistence in income and social class', p. 20. This would be a powerful argument, except that the difference in mobility rates comparing single-earner and dual-earner households is not very large. A further complication is that the increase in the number of working mothers between the 1958 and 1970 cohorts meant that household incomes became more *varied* in the period between the two studies (there is what statisticians call a higher 'variance' in the 1970 parental income data than in the comparable 1958 data, reflecting the increased impact of mothers' earnings). The 'coefficient of elasticity' (β), a key measure for assessing the relationship between parents' and sons' incomes, increases with increased variance. However, Blanden and her colleagues also used a second measure – the correlation coefficient (r)—which does not change with increasing variances, and this also strengthened between the two cohorts (although by a lesser degree).

[27] Robert Erikson and John Goldthorpe, 'Income and class mobility between generations in Great Britain', Equalsoc *Working Paper*, 2009/1.

[28] John Ermisch and Cheti Nicoletti, 'Intergenerational earnings mobility: Changes across cohorts in Britain' University of Essex, Institute for Social & Economic Research *Working Paper*, no. 19, 2005. This study estimates fathers' incomes for men in the sample aged 31-45 by looking at what older men in the sample were earning, correlating this with a number of indicators (occupational prestige score, managerial positions, formal qualifications, and age), and imputing from these indicators what fathers in the same generation were earning.

[29] Ermisch and Nicoletti, 'Intergenerational earnings mobility: Changes across cohorts in Britain', p. 27.

[30] There are a number of differences in the way incomes of parents were recorded in NCDS and BCS, and they all required adjustments to be made before joint parental incomes could be estimated. Not only did individual incomes in NCDS have to be aggregated to make them comparable with the total household income data collected in BCS, but total family income in BCS was recorded gross, while individual incomes in NCDS were recorded net, and the value of child benefit had to be imputed in BCS while it was included as 'other family income' in NCDS. The more the data had to be adjusted, the more scope for error.

[31] Blanden, Gregg and Macmillan, 'Intergenerational persistence in income and social class', p. 17.

[32] It is not always clear whether parents reported their normal, or their disrupted, incomes, although recorded incomes for NCDS parents in 1974 apparently correspond quite closely with Family Expenditure Survey data for the same period—see Dearden, Machin and Reed, 'Intergenerational mobility in Britain', p. 13.

[33] David Goodhart, 'More mobile than we think' *Prospect*, 20 December 2008.

4: What Would a Perfect Meritocracy Look Like?

[1] John Goldthorpe, *Social Mobility and Class Structure in Modern Britain*, second edn, Oxford: Clarendon Press, 1987, p. 114.

[2] Gordon Marshall, Howard Newby, David Rose and Carolyn Vogler, *Social Class in Modern Britain*, London: Hutchinson, 1988, p. 138.

[3] Stephen Aldridge, *Social Mobility: A Discussion Paper*, Cabinet Office Performance & Innovation Unit, April 2001, para 70.

[4] Cabinet Office Strategy Unit, *Getting On, Getting Ahead*, November 2008, pp. 24-25.

[5] John Hills and others, *An Anatomy of Economic Inequality in the UK*, London: Government Equalities Office, 2010, p. 2.

[6] *Hansard*, 11 June 2009, col.985. See also the Conservative Party, *Through the Glass Ceiling: A Conservative Agenda for Social Mobility*, p. 9.

[7] Michelle Jackson ('Non-meritocratic job requirements and the reproduction of class inequality' *Work, Employment & Society*, vol. 15, 2001, pp. 619-30) suggests on the basis of a content analysis of job advertisements that: 'It is clear that merit

characteristics are important for employers' (p. 624), and this is true at all occupational levels.

8   Gordon Marshall rejects this criticism, saying that his work has tried to take differences of education into account (see G. Marshall and A. Swift, 'Merit and Mobility: A reply to Peter Saunders', *Sociology*, vol. 30, 1996). But educational qualifications on their own are a poor measure of ability, and they fail to pick up on those bright individuals who achieve occupational success through routes other than credentialism.

9   Such an explanation will, he says, appeal only to 'latter-day Social Darwinists or Smilesians' Goldthorpe, *Social Mobility and Class Structure in Modern Britain*, p. 328.

10 When I first suggested that left-wing British sociologists had been blind to the possibility that the class system was recruiting on the basis of ability, Ray Pawson criticised my 'contemptible attack' from what he described as my 'new right' position. R. Pawson, 'Half-truths about bias', *Sociology*, vol. 24, 1990, p. 239. My original critique was published as 'Left-write in sociology', *Network*, vol. 43, 1989, pp. 4-5.

11 P. Bourdieu, 'The school as a conservative force' in J. Eggleston (ed.), *Contemporary Research in the Sociology of Education*, London: Methuen, 1974, p. 42.

12 S. Bowles and H. Gintis, 'IQ in the United States class structure' in A. Gartner, C. Greer and F. Riessman (eds), *The New Assault on Equality: IQ and social stratification*, New York: Harper Row, 1974, p. 33.

13 James Heckman, 'Lessons from the Bell Curve' *The Journal of Political Economy*, vol. 103, October 1995, p. 1092 .

14 The first stage of my work on social mobility was a three-month project funded by a small 'personal research grant' of just £7,740 from the Economic and Social Research Council. Small grants like this did not require peer review and did not have to go before the full Panel. After I submitted my final report on that project, the ESRC flagged it in its 1994/95 Annual Report as 'a major ESRC-funded study' (even though the funding was tiny in comparison with most of the grants given out by the Council). The ESRC also featured the project prominently in its press release, and put it on the front page of its March 1996 *Social Sciences* newsletter. The research was picked up by *The Independent*, the *Independent on Sunday*, the *Daily Telegraph*, the *Guardian* and the *Sunday Times*, and more than 40 local authorities and voluntary sector bodies (in addition to academics) contacted me asking for copies. The ESRC Deputy Head of External Relations wrote to me praising the 'extensive coverage' my research had received, and the External Relations Division wrote congratulating me on my

'extremely successful' project. Suitably encouraged, I submitted a further application to ESRC for more substantial funding so I could continue the work, but this application was turned down following negative referees' reports. I reworked it and applied again, this time with a psychology colleague, but the application was again turned down following even more hostile referees' reports. I wrote to the Chairman of ESRC expressing my suspicion that the application had been rejected for political reasons and asking him to investigate. He assured me that the application 'was considered by the Research Grants Board in open competition through the normal process of peer review... Reservations were expressed by [some] referees and by Board members [but]... I can find no evidence either of bad faith or of political interference' (Letter from Prof Bruce Smith, 10 May 1996). The fact remains that the first phase of the research, which did not go to peer review, was judged by ESRC to have been enormously successful, yet the proposed follow-up, which did go to peer review, was flatly rejected—not once, but twice.

[15] Hans Eysenck, *Rebel With a Cause*, London: W.H. Allen, 1990. In the mid-1990s, shortly before his death, I invited Eysenck to give a seminar to academics and graduate students at Sussex University, where I was teaching. All but three of my academic colleagues boycotted the talk.

[16] See *Times Higher Education Supplement*, 19 April 1996.

[17] See, for example, L. Kamin, 'Behind the curve', *Scientific American*, February 1995, who concludes that 'The book has nothing to do with science' (p. 86). See also A. Palmer, 'Does white mean right?', *The Spectator*, 18 February 1995, pp. 9-11), and the various contributions to *The Bell Curve Wars* edited by S. Fraser, New York: Basic Books, 1995.

[18] 'Whenever intelligence is said, "race" is heard', Daniel Casse, 'IQ since the Bell Curve', *Commentary*, August 1998.

[19] Adrian Wooldridge, *Meritocracy and the 'Classless Society'*, Social Market Foundation, 1995.

[20] See, for example, Brian Jackson and Dennis Marsden, *Education and the Working Class*, London: Routledge & Kegan Paul, 1962; Jack Douglas, *The Home and the School*, London: MacGibbon & Kee, 1964; Basil Bernstein, 'Education cannot compensate for society', *New Society*, 26 February 1970, pp. 344-7.

[21] H. Eysenck versus L. Kamin, *Intelligence: The battle for the mind*, London: Pan, 1981.

[22] A. Halsey, A. Heath, J. Ridge, *Origins and Destinations: Family, Class and Education in Modern Britain*, Oxford: Clarendon Press, 1980.

[23] Halsey, Heath and Ridge, *Origins and Destinations*, p. 209.

24 Anthony Heath, *Social Mobility*, Fontana, 1981, p. 165.

25 For a review from both sides of the debate, see Eysenck versus Kamin, *Intelligence*. Eysenck's contribution includes evidence on the internal and external reliability of IQ tests, and evidence drawn from work on reaction times and evoked potentials.

26 Heckman is scathing about the work of Kamin and Gould, two of the most influential critics of IQ research. He says they 'rely heavily on innuendo', they ignore the evidence on the predictive power of IQ scores, and they peddle the idea that IQ tests are culture-biased with little or no justification — 'Lessons from the Bell Curve', *The Journal of Political Economy*, p. 1096.

27 A raw correlation of 0.63 was adjusted up to 0.73 to take account of the attenuation of the sample, but the authors claim even this under-estimates the true strength of association, due to the effects of measurement error. See Ian Deary and others, 'The stability of individual differences in mental ability from childhood to old age', *Intelligence*, vol. 28, 2000, pp. 49-55.

28 The fact that IQ correlates with forward and backward digit span test results enables us to rule out differential motivation as a possible cause of variations in IQ scores, for subjects will be no less motivated calculating backward than forward sequences, but it is the latter that correlates with IQ: See Richard Herrnstein and Charles Murray, *The Bell Curve*, New York: Free Press, 1994.

29 See Herrnstein and Murray for a discussion of experiments based on forward and backward digit span tests and reaction time tests (pp. 282-86), and Hans Eysenck, 'Clever measures', *Times Higher Education Supplement*, 27 January 1995, for a discussion of positron emission topography. Much of this research is also reviewed by Daniel Casse, 'IQ since the Bell Curve' *Commentary*, who concludes that, 'General intelligence as a psychological trait is] on a more solid foundation than is enjoyed by any other aspect of personality or behaviour.'

30 Summarising the state of research, Nicholas Mackintosh suggests: 'There are distinctions between tests of verbal and spatial ability, abstract reasoning and speed of information processing, but... these tests all correlate positively with one another. It is, therefore, at best misleading to say that these tests measure wholly independent abilities. More plausibly, they measure a set of over-lapping processes whose importance varies from one kind of test to another. Whether there is a single, underlying process of general intelligence that is more important than the others is simply not known.' N. Mackintosh, 'Insight into intelligence', *Nature*, vol. 377, 19 October 1995, p. 582.

31 Eysenck guesses that 50 genes could eventually be found to be shaping intelligence; Herrnstein thinks it could be 100. See also Lucy Hodge's interview with Robert Plomin, *Times Higher Education Supplement*, 22 December 1995.

32 Lucy Hodge's interview with Robert Plomin, *Times Higher Education Supplement*, 22 December 1995.

33 Eysenck versus Kamin, *Intelligence*; Hans Eysenck, *The Inequality of Man*, London: Temple Smith, 1973; D. Fulker and H. Eysenck, *The Structure and Measurement of Intelligence*, New York: Springer-Verlag, 1979.

34 In Eysenck versus Kamin, *Intelligence*. Similar figures are reported in Richard Herrnstein, *IQ in the Meritocracy*, Boston: Little, Brown & Co, 1973, who also lists correlation coefficients for different types of blood relatives. Correlations are expressed by a coefficient, *r*, which varies between 0 (no correlation) and 1 (perfect correlation). By squaring a correlation coefficient, it is possible to calculate the proportion of variance in a dependent variable which is accounted for by the independent variable. For example, if variable X is thought to influence variable Y, and we find a correlation of 0.5 between them, we can say that X explains (0.5 x 0.5) = 0.25 of the variance in Y.

35 Heckman, 'Lessons from the Bell Curve', p. 1116.

36 For evidence on average IQ scores of children born to fathers and mothers with various different levels of IQ, see S. Preston and C. Campbell, 'Differential fertility and the distribution of traits: The case of IQ', *American Journal of Sociology*, vol. 98, 1993, pp. 997-1019, Table 2.

37 This material is summarised in Hills, *An Anatomy of Economic Inequality in the UK*, pp. 330-38.

38 A 'normal' distribution is one where most people score at or around the average for the whole population, and there is a consistent 'tailing off' in the number of people scoring above or below this point. Height is an obvious example of a normal distribution, for many people are within a few centimetres of the mean height of the whole population, and there are progressively fewer people at each height as we move further away on each side from this mid-point.

39 This reasoning seems to have informed Herrnstein's conclusion that inheritance of social positions will increase, the more meritocratic a society becomes, and it was the logic behind Halsey's belief that only just over one per cent of the children of a less intelligent lower class would achieve upward mobility in a pure meritocracy (A. Halsey, 'Genetics, social structure and intelligence' *British Journal of Sociology*, vol. 9, 1958, pp. 15-28). This reasoning may also have influenced Michael Young's gloomy prognosis about the emergence of a new dominant class in a meritocratic Britain of the future.

40 Eysenck (in Eysenck versus Kamin, *Intelligence*) cites work by Terman on a sample of 1528 exceptionally intelligent individuals, all of whom had an IQ of 140 or more, and whose average IQ score was 152. Most mated with partners

who also had a high IQ (average 125) producing a set of parents with an average IQ of 138.5. When their children were tested, however, the average IQ score was somewhat lower than this at 133.2. There had, in other words, been some regression to the mean. Similarly, Waller has found that middle class parents achieve average IQ scores of 114 while their children register a lower average of 109. By contrast, unskilled manual worker parents have an average IQ of 81 while their children score an average of 91 (cited in Eysenck, *The structure and Measurement of Intelligence*).

[41] As Eysenck puts it: 'Regression is intimately connected with social mobility... Regression mixes up the social classes, ensures social mobility and favours meritocracy' Eysenck versus Kamin, *Intelligence*, p. 64.

[42] Hans Eysenck, *The Inequality of Man*, London: Temple Smith, 1973, p. 139. I am indebted to Dr. Rod Bond for his work in calculating this coefficient from the data cited by Eysenck.

[43] Anna Christina d'Addio, 'Intergenerational transmission of disadvantage' OECD Employment & Migration *Working Papers* no. 52, 2007, p. 24. d'Addio adds that this does not necessarily indicate that IQ is genetically transmitted, although 0.5 is also, of course, the correlation which would be expected if IQ were based wholly on innate (genetic) intelligence (Herrnstein, *IQ in the Meritocracy*, chapter 4).

[44] Actual figures are taken from Goldthorpe's 1972 data coded according to his original class schema, taken from table 9.8.

5: Is Britain a Meritocracy?

[1] The analysis that follows is based on the 6,795 panel members who were still in the study at age 33 and who had full-time employment. Eighty-five per cent were employees and 15 per cent self-employed. Seventy per cent were male and 30 per cent female. Panel wastage has resulted in some under-representation of unskilled manual workers, but the bias is not thought to be serious. More details are provided in *Unequal But Fair?*, chapter 7, and in Peter Saunders, 'Social mobility in Britain: An empirical evaluation of two competing explanations' *Sociology*, vol. 31, 1997.

[2] We define the 'middle class' as classes I and II, comprising professionals, managers, administrators and employers; the 'lower working class' is classes IV and V, comprising semi- and unskilled manual workers; and classes IIIN and IIIM, comprising mainly routine white-collar and skilled manual workers, are defined as 'intermediate classes'.

[3] A similar conclusion emerges if we look at income mobility, controlling for ability. Paul Johnson and Howard Reed, ('Two nations? The inheritance of

poverty and affluence', Institute for Fiscal Studies *Commentary*, No. 53, 1996) take maths scores at age 7 as their measure of ability, and they report a 'fairly strong' correlation between children's scores on that simple test and their subsequent move, up or down, relative to the incomes of their parents. In particular, 'Bright children do seem to have a better chance of escaping low incomes' (p. 19).

4   At the age of 16, panel members were asked to respond (on a 5-point scale from strongly disagree to strongly agree) to eight comments about their experience of school: that school is largely a waste of time, that they get on with their classwork, that homework is boring, that they cannot keep their mind on their work, that they do not take the work seriously, that they dislike school, that they see no point going on to further study, and that they are willing to help their teachers. Their answers were combined into a single 'motivation index' by scoring one point on each item where they were strongly negative about school, through to five points where they were strongly positive. Further details can be found at:
http://www.cls.ioe.ac.uk/datadictionary/page.asp?section=0001000100010004000
10005&sectionTitle=E+%2D+Attitude+to+School

5   In the original NCDS data, low scores on the motivation scale indicate high motivation. Because this is counter-intuitive, and hence potentially confusing, the scale has been reversed here.

6    $F=131.0$ with 5 degrees of freedom.

7   In a simple least squares regression model, we plot two variables against each other on a scatter graph and draw a straight line through the points so that it minimises the distance of each point from the line (because some points are below the line – which makes them negative values—we 'square' all the distances above and below the line so we can add them all together, which is why it is called a 'least squares' regression). The resulting graph can be expressed as an equation of the form $Y = a + bX$, where Y is the value on the y (vertical) axis, a is the 'constant' (the point on the y axis where the line intersects), and b is the slope of the line (i.e. the number of units by which Y changes for each unit change in the value of X). Although we cannot draw it on a two-dimensional graph, it is possible to expand this basic regression equation to encompass more than one independent variable. Thus: $Y = a + b_1X_1 + b_2X_2 + b_3X_3...$ This is known as a 'multiple regression model'.

8   See John Goldthorpe and Keith Hope, *The Social Grading of Occupations*, Oxford: Clarendon Press, 1974. This scale is used because it provides a dependent variable measured at interval level. This enables multivariate analysis based on least squares regression and the development of a path model derived from structural equation models. Goldthorpe himself abandoned this scale (in favour

of a categorical class schema) when he applied log-linear modelling techniques to the analysis of social mobility tables, but regression-based models remain more appropriate if the concern is to understand how different individuals end up in different positions, as opposed to Goldthorpe's major concern with analysing the effects of relative mobility rates on class structuration. For a discussion of these issues, see the papers by Kelley and Marshall, together with Goldthorpe's reply, in J. Clark, C. Modgil and S. Modgil (eds), *John H Goldthorpe: Consensus and Controversy*, London: Falmer Press, 1990.

9   Variables entered/deleted stepwise with $p<0.05$ as criterion for entry and $p>0.10$ as criterion for deletion. Missing data replaced by group means based on gender.

10   The model presented here was developed with my colleague, Dr. Rod Bond, to whom I am most grateful for the huge amount of work which he put in to producing it. It was published in our joint paper, Rod Bond and Peter Saunders, 'Routes of success: Influences on the occupational attainment of young British males', *British Journal of Sociology*, vol. 50, 1999.

11   There are various measures of the degree to which a model like this fits the data. All are expressed on a scale from zero to 1, and convention dictates that the degree of fit should exceed 0.90. In the model outlined in figure 1, the Goodness of Fit index equals 0.975—a very high degree of fit for a model of this complexity.

12   It should be noted that, as we move through the path diagram, the coefficients relating to later variables express only their additional effect, not necessarily their total effect. Ability at 16, for example, has a loading of only 0.11 on qualifications achieved at 16, but we see that ability at 11 also loads directly on qualifications at 16 with a Beta of 0.34. The coefficient of 0.11 gives us the *additional* effect of ability at 16, after the effect of ability at 11 has been taken fully into account.

13   All research on class destinations ends up with a large proportion of variance unexplained. In his review of the literature, Aldridge (*Social Mobility: A Discussion Paper*, Cabinet Office Performance & Innovation Unit, April 2001, para 40) notes that models rarely exceed 25 per cent of variance explained, so 35 per cent is comparatively strong. This failure to explain much of the variance partly reflects error in the measurement of the variables, and is partly due to the influence of factors we cannot measure, such as luck and personal idiosyncrasies.

6: How Robust are the Research Findings?

1   For example: Gordon Marshall and Adam Swift, 'Merit and mobility: A reply to
     Peter Saunders', *Sociology* 30, 1996, pp. 375-86; Mike Savage and M. Egerton,
     'Social mobility, individual ability and the inheritance of class inequality',
     Sociology 31, 1997, pp. 645-72.

2   R. Breen and J. Goldthorpe, 'Class inequality and meritocracy: A critique of
     Saunders and an alternative analysis,' *British Journal of Sociology* 50,1999, pp. 1-
     27; R. Breen and J. Goldthorpe, 'Class mobility and merit: The experience of two
     British birth cohorts', *European Sociological Review* vol.17, 2001, 81-101; R. Breen
     and J. Goldthorpe, 'Merit, mobility and method: Another reply to Saunders'
     British Journal of Sociology 53, 2002, pp. 575-82.

3   Breen and Goldthorpe (1999) say that I 'disregard a large body of relevant
     literature' (p. 6), I should have been 'better acquainted with obviously relevant
     literature' (p. 8), I need to 're-read' the literature on IQ (footnote 10); and my
     'disregard' of earlier studies 'is conspicuous (footnote 21). They also question
     my methodological competence: I do not 'securely grasp the "logic" of odds
     ratios' (p. 5); I 'ignore' the complexity in interpreting regression models (p. 7); I
     'introduced biases' in my measures to favour my own position (p. 21); I use
     'undesirable' and 'ad hoc' procedures for dealing with missing cases (footnote
     9); and my methodology is 'biased' (p. 8).

4   R. Breen and J. Goldthorpe, 'Merit, mobility and method', fn.1.

5   *Social Mobility and Class Structure in Modern Britain*, p. 328. In his later work
     with Breen, Goldthorpe denies that he ever advocated the SAD thesis,
     suggesting it has only been his intention to reject the meritocracy thesis. Given
     his comment in his earlier book (p. 328) that 'no significant reduction in class
     inequalities [has been] achieved,' this is disingenuous, for he clearly equates
     high odds ratios with the operation of 'inequalities rooted in the class structure.'

6   'In his empirical work Saunders does tend to focus on just one half of the
     picture: that is, on disparity ratios that pertain to upward rather than to
     downward mobility chances. There is, of course, no justification for this
     partiality, and it can—and indeed in certain circumstances does—prove
     misleading' (Breen and Goldthorpe, 'Class inequality and meritocracy', p. 4).

7   It is actually doubtful whether this had much of an effect on my results, for the
     two schema correlate closely when collapsed into just three categories.
     Analysing their occupations in 1974 (when the NCDS children were aged 16), 84
     per cent of the fathers in Goldthorpe's service class were coded to Registrar
     General classes I/II in my analysis; 78 per cent of those in Goldthorpe's
     intermediate and skilled manual classes were coded to Registrar General class
     IIIn/IIIm in my analysis; and 98 per cent of those in Goldthorpe's bottom class

were coded to Registrar General class IV/V in my analysis. Treating both schema as ordinal scales produces a correlation between them (Spearman's Rho) of 0.782 (p <0.001).

[8] 'Dummy variables' have just two values, 0 and 1. If a certain condition is met (e.g. if a person is a member of the service class), the value is 1; otherwise (e.g. if they belong to any other class) the value is 0. Dummy variables can be used in multiple regression models to replace variables which are not measured on an interval scale, and which cannot therefore be used in regression equations. Goldthorpe's classes are one such variable, for he insists that the classes in his schema cannot even be ranked ordinally (other than in the division between the service class and the rest). This is why, in my original modelling, I chose to use the Registrar General schema, which I crunched into 3 broad values which I treated as an equal-interval scale. Breen and Goldthorpe claim that, by crunching this schema into three categories, I deliberately limited its potential explanatory power. This is not the case, for I drew the boundaries between the classes in such a way as to sharpen as far as possible the divisions of income, status, autonomy and power between them. Nevertheless, it is possible that estimating class effects through a set of dummy variables may result in a stronger association than is possible by using a single linear variable with one degree of freedom, so I have re-run the models on this basis. In Table 16, six of Goldthorpe's classes are entered as dummy variables (class VII is omitted as, when using dummy variables, one value has to be omitted given that its effects will already have been taken into account in the combined effects of all the others).

[9] In my early work analysing the NCDS data, I measured *ability* using the same variable that Breen and Goldthorpe use in their subsequent re-analysis (variable N920). This records the scores achieved by respondents on an 80 item test taken at age 11. Also, like Breen and Goldthorpe, I measured *motivation* using variable N1760 which is based on answers at age 16 to a series of attitude questions about school. Unlike them, however, I also derived two further measures of motivation: 'absenteeism' (a behavioural factor based on school truancy and attendance records), and 'work attitudes' (based on responses to three questions about work asked when respondents were aged 33). In my later work with Rod Bond, we constructed more complex latent measures of both ability and motivation. *Ability* was measured at three different ages using arithmetic test scores, reading comprehension test scores and teacher ratings as well as the results of the general ability test at age 11, and *motivation* at age 16 was measured by a single factor created from the weighted loadings of teacher ratings, truancy data and trivial absenteeism data, as well as scores on the Academic Motivation Scale.

Breen and Goldthorpe are highly critical of all of this. As regards my earlier work, they attack my use of absenteeism data on the grounds that trivial absences do not indicate disenchantment with schooling, and they criticize my use of work attitudes at age 33 on the grounds that these do not predate people's occupational attainment and cannot therefore be included as possible causal influences upon it. In fact, truancy is a plausible behavioural indicator of low motivation at school, but to appease them, we can drop it, along with the work attitudes at age 33. The key point to remember about both of these measures is that they were used in my analysis *in addition to* the variables which Breen and Goldthorpe favour. It is difficult to see how including these additional measures can be said to have 'biased' my results. They think that attempting to create more robust and reliable measures by using several different indicators is 'inappropriate' ('Class inequality and meritocracy', p. 21), and that an approach which uses only one measure of ability (the general test result at age 11) and only one measure of motivation (the attitude score at age 16) is to be preferred as somehow more valid and reliable. This is a strange argument, for use of multiple indicators is a standard procedure for minimizing measurement error. However, in the interests of finding common ground, I revert in my re-analysis to use of the simpler measures that they prefer. We shall see that it makes little difference to the final result.

¹⁰ Significance levels: * <0.05, ** <0.01, *** <0.001. N=6795 (missing cases are replaced by mean values grouped by gender). *Father's class* is measured on the Goldthorpe 7-class schema as a set of dummy variables with Class VII as comparison, and is based on father's occupation in 1974, or in 1969 if not employed in 1974. It has been derived from data on father's SEG as recommended by M. Savage and M. Egerton, 'Social mobility, individual ability and the inheritance of class inequality', *Sociology* 31,1997, p. 651. *Parents' education* measures whether none, one or both parents stayed at school beyond the minimum leaving age and is derived from variables n194 and n537. *Parental contact with school* is a 4 point scale measuring whether either parent visited the child's school at ages 7, 11 and 16, and is derived from variables n41, n849 and n2322 (it is preferred to other possible indicators of parental interest in the child's education, such as teacher evaluations, because it is behavioural and it has a relatively low number of missing cases). *Parents read to child age 7* is a 6 point scale derived from variables n179 and n180. *Overcrowding in parental home* measures occupants per room at ages 7, 11 and 16 and is derived from variables n607, n1683 and n1734. *Home lacked basic amenities* measures access to basic amenities in the parental home at ages 7, 11 and 16 and is derived from variables n621, n1681 and n1736. *Pre-school education* and *Private education* are both dummy variables derived from n105/ n106/n107 and n2103 respectively. *Ability test score, age 11* is the score on a 40 item verbal and 40 item non-verbal IQ-style test (n920). *Motivation score, age 16* is based on answers to 8 attitude

items (n1760). *School exam results* is a rising scale of number and grade of CSE, GCE 'O' and GCE 'A' levels (plus Scottish equivalents) achieved by age 19 and is derived from variables e385, e389, e397 and e405. *Post-school qualifications* is a scale based on NVQ equivalence and referring only to qualifications gained post-school leaving; it is calculated from n501441, taking account of data on school examinations.

[11] The regression model in Table 13 explained a higher proportion of the variance (32 per cent). The fall is partly because fewer variables have been included this time round, but is also because the merit variables are more crudely measured (as a result of adopting Breen and Goldthorpe's preferred measures), thereby increasing measurement error.

[12] Savage and Egerton, 'Social mobility, individual ability and the inheritance of class inequality', report similar calculations on the same data set, with odds ratios at least halving when ability is taken into account.

[13] 'Class inequality and meritocracy', p. 17. Breen and Goldthorpe's model does not directly measure the effect of class origins on class destinations, but much of the unexplained co-variation that remains after 'merit' has been taken into account is undoubtedly due to measurement error and the effect of other variables not included in the model, rather than to the influence of class. Our regression modelling indicates that, when we do measure the 'class origin effect' directly, it is actually quite small.

[14] Breen and Goldthorpe make much of the fact that qualifications explain more than ability and motivation, and they seem to think that this undermines my argument about the importance of ability. But the effect of qualifications in itself supports neither the meritocracy nor SAD hypotheses since neither thesis denies that qualifications are important (while the latter sees qualifications as a product of class-bias in education, the former sees them as the result of ability and effort). However, the path model demonstrates that qualifications are more a product of ability and effort than of class origins. Furthermore, because ability and motivation are logically prior to the achievement of qualifications, they should clearly be included *before* qualifications in any model. Breen and Goldthorpe, however, enter qualifications first. It is also important to recognize that ability continues to exert a substantial independent effect on occupational success, even *after* qualifications are taken into account. As the path model makes clear, bright people achieve a higher position than their less able contemporaries at all levels of qualification.

[15] Savage and Egerton, for example, conclude: 'Those who do well in ability tests from any social class background have reasonable chances of moving into advantaged jobs' ('Social mobility, individual ability and the inheritance of class inequality', p. 664).

[16] Model 1 is based on change in R^2 statistics in Table 16 (total variance explained = 27 per cent). Model 2 is based on change in R^2 in a regression model using the same variables but where ability and motivation are entered first, exam results and post-school qualifications are entered second, father's class is entered third (as six dummy variables) and the remaining variables are entered last. Model 3 is based on the path model (total variance explained = 35 per cent), and the Breen and Goldthorpe findings (model 4) are based on their 1999 paper (percentage reductions in odds ratios calculated on reductions from 20.7 to 11.1 to 7.4 for men, and from 16.3 to 6.3 to 3.3 for women).

[17] David Nettle, 'Intelligence and class mobility in the British population' *British Journal of Psychology*, vol. 94, 2003, 551-61.

[18] According to Breen and Goldthorpe, 'Children of less advantaged origins need to show substantially more "merit" —however understood—than do children from more advantaged origins in order to enter similarly desirable positions' 'Class, mobility and merit', p. 82. Nettle's is not the only study to refute this: Ian Deary and his colleagues similarly find in a lifetime study of a sample of Scottish men born in 1921 that upwardly mobile men entering classes I and II from classes III, IV and V all have similar IQ scores to each other, which are somewhat lower than the average scores of men who were born into, and remained in, classes I and II. See Ian Deary et al., Intergenerational social mobility and mid-life status attainment' *Intelligence*, vol. 33, 2005, pp. 455-72.

[19] Nettle, 'Intelligence and class mobility in the British population', p. 560.

[20] Leon Feinstein, 'The relative economic importance of academic, psychological and behavioural attributes developed in childhood', London School of Economics *Centre for Economic Performance Papers*, no. 443, 2000.

[21] Sophie von Stumm, Catherine Gale, G. David Batty, Ian Deary, 'Childhood intelligence, locus of control and behaviour disturbance as determinants of intergenerational social mobility' *Intelligence*, vol. 37, 2009, p. 327.

[22] See, for example, Stephen Machin and Anna Vignoles, 'Educational inequality: The widening socio-economic gap' *Fiscal Studies*, vol. 25, 2004, pp. 107-28; Paul Gregg and Lindsey Macmillan, 'Access to education and basic skills' (In Simon Griffiths (ed.), *The Politics of Aspiration*, London: Social market Foundation, April 2007.

[23] Ingrid Schoon, 'A transgenerational model of status attainment' *National Institute Economic Review*, No. 205, 2008, p. 81.

[24] Gary Marks and Julie McMillan, 'Declining inequality?' *British Journal of Sociology*, vol. 54, 2003, pp. 53-71.

25 Fernando Galindo-Rueda and Anna Vignoles, *The Declining Relative Importance of Ability in predicting educational attainment*, London School of Economics, Centre for the Economics of Education, October 2003, p. 13. The authors believe that the move to comprehensive education may have reduced the importance of intelligence in obtaining qualifications, for in the 1958 cohort, brighter students from all backgrounds did better if they attended grammar schools. By abolishing 11+, we reduced selection by ability.

26 Stephen Machin and Anna Vignoles, 'Educational inequality: The widening socioeconomic gap', *Fiscal Studies*, vol. 25, 2004, pp. 107-28, Table 4.

27 Ian Deary, Michelle Taylor, Carole Hart, Valerie Wilson, George Smith, David Blane, John Starr, 'Intergenerational social mobility and mid-life status attainment' *Intelligence*, vol. 33, 2005, pp. 455-72.

28 Wendy Johnson, Ian Deary, William Iacono, 'Genetic and environmental transactions underlying educational attainment' *Intelligence*, vol. 37, 2009, pp. 466-78.

29 Fernando Galindo-Rueda and Anna Vignoles, *Class Ridden or Meritocratic? An economic analysis of recent changes in Britain*, London School of Economics Centre for the Economics of Education, May 2003, p. 32.

30 'Intelligence and socioeconomic success' *Intelligence*, vol. 35, 2007, p. 415.

31 'The role of ability needs to be acknowledged in any theorizing on social reproduction and occupational mobility' (Marks and McMillan, 'Declining inequality?', pp.467-68.

32 Sophie von Stumm, Catherine Gale, G David Batty, Ian Deary, 'Childhood intelligence, locus of control and behaviour disturbance as determinants of intergenerational mobility', *Intelligence*, vol. 37, 2009, pp. 329-40.

33 Jen Lexmond and Richard Reeves, *Building Character*, London: Demos, 2009.

34 Institute for Public Policy Research, *Social Mobility: A background review* (Prepared for the Liberal Democrats Commission on Social Mobility) April 2008, p. 14.

7: Policy Responses: Faint Hopes, False Starts and Red Herrings

1 Cabinet Office Strategy Unit, *Getting On, Getting Ahead*, November 2008, p. 15.

2 Getting On, Getting Ahead, p. 24.

3 *Unleashing Aspiration: The final report of the panel on fair access to the professions* (the Milburn Report), 2009, p. 27.

4   The discussion of intelligence is limited to half a page (p. 43). The report rejects 'the notion that the disparities observed in who gets into top careers are a product *purely* of inherited intelligence' (my emphasis), but this is engaging with a straw man, for nobody argues that intelligence explains *everything*. It then approvingly cites Breen and Goldthorpe's 2001 paper, claiming this proves that, 'While ability and effort do play a part, the effect of class origins on class destinations is, in fact, much stronger.' In fact, however, Breen and Goldthorpe's results do not show this, and even they do not make such a claim. Indeed, as we saw in chapter VI, Breen and Goldthorpe explicitly reject any attempt to 'set up a variable race' which might measure the relative effects of intelligence and class origins, so the report is wholly misleading in the interpretation it draws from their work. Its discussion then ends back where it began: 'Were opportunities...truly meritocratic, we would expect to see substantially more social mobility.' But nobody argues the system is entirely meritocratic. Like Goldthorpe, this report sets up a straw man ('pure meritocracy'), shows that the reality stops short of the perfect ideal, and assumes that this is enough to dispense with the thesis altogether.

5   Children whose mothers have GCSE passes are about 4 months ahead of the norm for their age; those whose mothers have A-levels are 6 months ahead; and those with graduate mothers are almost 8 months ahead. John Hills and others, *An Anatomy of Economic Inequality in the UK*, London: Government Equalities Office, 2010, p. 338.

6   In a Swedish study, the years of education of biological, step and adoptive parents were compared with the years of education undertaken by their children. The study found a stronger correlation between biological parents and children, *even when the parent had been entirely absent from the child's upbringing* (Anders Bjorkland, Markus Jantii and Gary Solon, 'Nature and nurture in the intergenerational transmission of socioeconomic status', *The B.E. Journal of Economic Analysis and Policy*, vol. 7, 2007, article 4). This strongly suggests, not only that genetic transmission is important in determining educational attainment, but also that years of education vary with genetically-based intelligence.

7   Hills, *An Anatomy of Economic Inequality in the UK*, p. 386.

8   Herrnstein and Murray point out that, with perhaps one-third of IQ being determined by environmental factors, it should be possible, at least in theory, to raise the cognitive functioning of children born into the least advantaged homes. Foetal development can be influenced by, for example, getting mothers to stop drinking alcohol or smoking cigarettes during pregnancy, and we know that higher birth weights correlate positively with later IQ scores. Changes to

early parenting styles might also pay dividends. See Richard Herrnstein and Charles Murray, *The Bell Curve*, New York: Free Press, 1994, chapter 17

9   Michael Hanlon 'Let's not be dumb about stupidity', *Spectator* 12 March 2005, pp. 18-19.

10 Research at Durham University has for 20 years compared students' A-level results with their performance on standardised tests. It finds that A-level grade standards have slipped by about 10 per cent of a grade each year. This means that someone who got a B grade in 1997 could expect to get an A grade today. Jack Grimston, 'The £100 billion schools scandal', *The Sunday Times* 24 January 2010.

11 See Fred Hirsch, *Social Limits to Growth*, Cambridge MA: Harvard University Press, 1976.

12 Grimston, 'The £100 billion schools scandal'; Polly Curtis, 'How target of 50% going to university foundered' *Guardian*, 20 August 2009; Higher Education Funding Council for England, *Trends in young participation in higher education* HEFCE, January 2010.

13 Blanden and Machin, 'Up and down the generational income ladder in Britain' *National Institute Economic Review*, No.205, 2008, p. 110.

14 Gosta Esping-Andersen, 'Social inheritance and equal opportunities policies', in Simone Delorenzi, Jodie Reed and Peter Robinson (eds), *Maintaining Momentum: Promoting social mobility and life chances from early years to adulthood*, London: IPPR, 2005.

15 Esping-Andersen, 'Social inheritance and equal opportunities policies', p. 24.

16 *Getting On, Getting Ahead*, p. 70.

17 83 of the 88 suggestions have been accepted by the government, although Milburn's most radical suggestion (a proposal to give disadvantaged children enhanced-value school vouchers to enable them to gain entry to better schools outside their neighbourhoods) was swiftly rejected by the Prime Minister—see Rachel Sylvester, 'Class war is so last week for new Gordon', *The Times* 19 January 2010.

18 *Unleashing Aspiration*, p. 32. The report also worries that vocational training has less kudos than a university degree, but is often the preferred route for working class children. Its desire to dragoon more of them into university degree courses is another example of Dench's concern that successful, middle class Labour politicians have lost regard for non-academic forms of work and qualification.

19 John Goldthorpe and Colin Mills, 'Trends in intergenerational class mobility in modern Britain', *National Institute Economic Review*, no. 205, 2008, 83-100.

20 Tellingly, the Association of Graduate Recruiters, representing 750 major employers, has called on the government to abandon its aim of getting 50 per cent of young people into higher education, arguing that this target has pushed too many students onto 'substandard courses' (Graeme Paton, 'Majority of graduates "only fit for Starbucks"', *Daily Telegraph* 11 March 2010).

21 *Getting On, Getting Ahead*, p. 60.

22 *Unleashing Aspiration*, p. 38.

23 Trevor Noble, 'The mobility transition: Social mobility trends in the first half of the 21st century', *Sociology*, vol. 34, 2000.

24 John Goldthorpe and Michelle Jackson, 'Intergenerational class mobility in contemporary Britain', *British Journal of Sociology*, vol. 58, 2007, p. 541.

25 Peter Hoskin, 'The widening public-private divide', *Spectator* blog, 1 February 2010; http://www.spectator.co.uk/coffeehouse/5744598/the-widening-publicprivate-divide.thtml

26 Goldthorpe and Jackson, 'Intergenerational class mobility in contemporary Britain', p. 542.

27 Stephen Aldridge, *Social Mobility: A Discussion Paper*, Cabinet Office Performance & Innovation Unit, April 2001, para 16.

28 See, for example, Harry Brighouse and Adam Swift, 'Legitimate parental partiality' University of Oxford, Dept of Politics and International relations *Working Paper* SJ002, October 2006.

29 Brighton and Hove was the first education authority to move to a lottery system for allocating children to secondary schools. Some of the economists who believe that social mobility has been falling have also expressed support for lotteries and bussing as a way of countering this (e.g. Paul Gregg and Lindsey Macmillan, 'Access to education and basic skills' in Simon Griffiths (ed.), *The Politics of Aspiration*, London: Social market Foundation, April 2007, p. 46).

30 In its paper on social mobility, prepared for the Liberal Democrat Party, the Institute for Public Policy Research warns: 'Be cautious about ability group teaching—which can damage the performance of children from lower social classes', IPPR, *Social Mobility: A background review*, April 2008, p. 20.

31 The 2006 Charities Act requires independent schools to demonstrate a 'public benefit' in order to maintain their tax-exempt charitable status. The Charities Commission interpreted this to mean that schools should offer a large (but

unspecified) number of free bursaries, and in its first round of assessments, it 'failed' two of the five schools it considered because they did not 'ensure that people in poverty are not excluded from the opportunity to benefit' (BBC News, 13 July 2009; http://news.bbc.co.uk/1/hi/education/8148347.stm). Effectively, independent schools are being forced to raise their fees to middle class parents in order to cover the cost of more free places for working class children, although the Commission announced in October that they will be given more time to make these adjustments (Chris Harris, 'Independent schools to keep tax breaks after charity chief backs down', *The Times* 8 October 2009).

[32] The Milburn report complains (p. 89) that 'the difference in the participation rate [of students from different backgrounds] at more selective universities remains very wide' and it recommends that universities should 'monitor' their intakes and offer lower grade entry requirements to applicants from lower socioeconomic origins (p. 92). Although it rejects quotas, it says: 'There is a strong case for universities to use data that takes account of the educational and social context of pupils' achievement' (recommendation 41 on p. 94). Business Secretary, Lord Mandelson agrees with this. Mandelson says: 'No one should be discriminated against or penalised on the basis of the family they come from, or the schools they attended' (quoted in James Kirkup, 'Middle class with A levels? It may not give you a university place' *Daily Telegraph*, 4 November 2009). He apparently fails to see the contradiction when he then goes on to propose that university tuition fees should vary for students from different social backgrounds, and that university admissions should be tweaked to favour of lower class candidates (one idea is that they should be given a two grade 'head start' over applicants from more privileged backgrounds)—see Jack Grimston, 'Mandelson to favour poor pupils' *The Sunday Times*, 9 August 2009. The former Vice Chancellor of Manchester University, Sir Martin Harris, has been asked to find ways to achieve this.

[33] Writing from a self-consciously 'centre-left' perspective, for example, Will Paxton and Mike Dixon (*The State of the Nation: An audit of injustice in the UK*, London, IPPR, 2004, p. 33) note: 'The centre-left should not necessarily want to fashion a purely meritocratic society: equality of opportunity may trade off against other objectives such as social cohesion and solidarity.' A similar argument can, of course, also be made from the 'centre-right' regarding the sacrifice of individual liberties and the attack on parents' rights which many of these proposals entail.

[34] The Sutton Trust recently complained that top universities draw entrants disproportionately from 200 leading schools, and suggested that universities should be required to reserve places for applicants from less successful state schools and poorer families. Jack Grimston, 'Labour curbs fail to loosen grip of middle class on top universities' *The Sunday Times*, 31 January 2010.

35 Hills, *An Anatomy of Economic Inequality in the UK*, p. 403.

36 Jo Blanden, 'How much can we learn from international comparisons of intergenerational mobility?', London School of Economics Centre for Economics of Education *Departmental Paper* November 2009, p. 15.

37 Esping-Andersen, 'Social inheritance and equal opportunities policies'.

38 *Unleashing Aspiration*, p. 28. See also *Getting On, Getting Ahead*, p. 89.

39 I have discussed this in more detail in Peter Saunders, 'Poverty of ambition: why we need a new approach to tackling child poverty' Policy Exchange, *Research Note*, October 2009.

40 Quoted in Marie Woolf, 'How £100 can boost child's ability' *The Sunday Times*, 24 January 2010.

41 David Goodhart, 'More mobile than we think', *Prospect*, 20 December 2008.

42 E.g. Department for Children, Schools and Families, *16-18 year olds NEET* December 2009; http://www.dcsf.gov.uk/14-19/index.cfm?go=site.home&sid=42&pid=343&ctype=None&ptype=Contents

43 I have discussed the concept of 'social exclusion' in Peter Saunders and Kayoko Tsumori, 'Poor Concepts: Social Exclusion, Poverty and the Politics of Guilt', *Policy*, Winter 2002.

44 See, for example, Charles Murray, *The Emerging British Underclass*, Institute of Economic Affairs, 1990; Charles Murray, *Underclass: the crisis deepens* Institute of Economic Affairs, 1994; Charles Murray, *Underclass +10* Civitas, 2001.

45 Alan Buckingham, 'Is there an underclass in Britain?', *British Journal of Sociology*, vol. 50, 1999, pp. 49-75.

46 Paul Johnson and Howard Reed, 'Two nations? The inheritance of poverty and affluence', Institute for Fiscal Studies, *Commentary*, No. 53, 1996.

47 Jen Lexmond and Richard Reeves, *Building Character*, London, Demos, 2009.

48 Institute for Public Policy Research, *Social Mobility: A background review*, April 2008, pp.14,13.

49 This is not without irony, for the key nineteenth century figure to emphasise the importance of character virtues was Samuel Smiles (see, for example, David Green, *Community Without Politics*, Institute of Economic Affairs, 1996, chapter 5). Smiles has for years been a figure or hate and ridicule on the left, so much so that when John Goldthorpe wanted to tarnish the idea that unequal achievements by children from different classes might reflect 'differing genetic, moral or other endowments,' he dismissed it as 'Smilesian' (*Social Mobility and*

Class Structure in Modern Britain, p. 328). It now seems that it is precisely these 'endowments' which left-wing policy advisers want to boost.

50 Esping-Andersen, 'Social inheritance and equal opportunities policies'.

51 Peter Saunders, *Reforming the UK Family Tax and Benefits System*, Policy Exchange, 2009.

52 OECD, *Babies and Bosses*, Paris, 2007, p. 78.

53 Peter Saunders, 'From entitlement to employment' in Lawrence Kay and Oliver Hartwich (eds), *When Hassle Means Help*, Policy Exchange, 2008.

54 Former Minister for Welfare Reform, Frank Field, points out that unconditional payments are fairly recent: 'For most of the last 400 years the receipt of welfare has been dependent on fulfilling a series of conditions. Only since the 1960s did an opposing idea gain ground…[the] damaging belief that no matter how badly a person behaves the right to welfare is inviolate.' (*Neighbours from Hell*, Politico's 2003, pp.33,95,98). He believes the failure to attach requirements to receipt of public funds is positively damaging: "Unconditional welfare declares that no behaviour is so out of bounds that the right to a minimum income is foregone. Taking away the assumption that welfare will always be paid irrespective of a claimant's behaviour is a crucial part of any successful strategy to re-establish common decencies.' (*The ethic of respect: A left-wing cause*, Centre for Independent Studies, Occasional Paper 102, 2006, pp. 40-42).

55 The Maternity Grant is worth £500 and is paid on the birth of a new child to families on welfare and to working families on low incomes.

56 *Unleashing Aspiration*, p. 29.

57 For a review of evidence from Britain and overseas, see Catherine Hakim, Karen Bradley, Emily Price and Louisa Mitchell, *Little Britons: Financing childcare choice*, Policy Exchange, 2008, chapter 2.

58 *Little Britons*, p. 46.

59 This proposal is broadly consistent with that advanced by David Green, *Individualists Who Cooperate* (Civitas 2009). At the time of writing (March 2010), the Labour government has suggested that single parents on Income Support should be expected to become 'job-ready' before their children start school, but this falls some way short of what is being proposed here, and the Conservatives have rejected even this modest proposal ('We do not support, and would not implement Government proposals to extend the requirement to prepare for work to lone parents of pre-school children' — *Through the Glass Ceiling: A Conservative Agenda for Social Mobility*, p. 27).

60 Conservative Party, *Through the Glass ceiling*, p. 3.

Appendix: Do We *Really* Want to Live in a Meritocracy?

1   *Unleashing Aspiration: The final report of the panel on fair access to the professions* (the Milburn Report), 2009, p. 9.

2   John Hills and others, *An Anatomy of Economic Inequality in the UK*, London: Government Equalities Office, 2010, p.v

3   Emile Durkheim, *The Division of Labour in Society*, London: Macmillan, 1933.

4   *The Division of Labour in Society*, pp. 375-7.

5   I have reviewed this theory in more detail in Peter Saunders, *Social Class and Stratification*, London: Routledge, 1990.

6   Michael Young, 'Looking back on *Meritocracy*' in Geoff Dench (ed.), *The Rise and Rise of Meritocracy*, Blackwell Publishing, 2006, p. 74.

7   Richard Herrnstein and Charles Murray, *The Bell Curve*, New York: Free Press, 1994, p. 522.

8   R.Turner, 'Sponsored and contest mobility and the school system', *American Sociological Review*, vol. 25, 1960.

9   One of the ironies in all this is that a principal argument which used to be put against educational selection at eleven was that it was socially divisive and emotionally fraught for those who failed to achieve a place in the grammar schools. The move to comprehensive secondary education has almost certainly made this problem worse, however, for the less able students are (in theory at least) now kept within sight and reach of the brightest throughout their school careers, only to fall to the wayside at sixteen. In reality, of course, many of them jump before they are pushed, which may help explain why there is such a huge problem of truancy, disruption and disaffection in the British comprehensive school system today. Similarly in higher education, disillusionment and cynicism of students may well result from the dawning recognition that despite clutching a lower-second degree from a new university, the glittering prizes are still out of reach. Problems of legitimation and social cohesion are likely to be much greater in a society which gives half of its young people degrees and then offers them jobs as shop assistants than in one which degrees are limited in the first place.

10   Robert Merton, 'Contributions to the theory of reference group behavior' in his *Social Theory and Social Structure,* New York: Free Press, 1957. Merton bases his analysis on the book by S. A. Stouffer and his colleagues, *The American Soldier: Adjustments during army life,* Princeton University Press, 1949. On the importance of comparative reference groups for feelings of relative deprivation,

see also W.G. Runciman, *Relative Deprivation and Social Justice*, London: Routledge & Kegan Paul, 1966.

[11] A good example is Polly Toynbee's attack on my initial research findings in the *Independent on Sunday*, 17 December 1995. Toynbee thought the very idea that social mobility might be a product of innate intelligence was 'lethally dangerous', and she dismissed my research findings as ideology masked by a 'veneer of science'. In place of my findings, she considered it was self-evident (as 'any pushy parent knows') that intelligence can be dramatically changed by parental intervention. In fact, as the path model in chapter VI demonstrates, parental ambition for children has virtually no impact on their IQ level.

[12] Daniel Bell, *The Coming of Post-Industrial Society*, London, Heinemann, 1974.

[13] A. Halsey, A. Heath, J. Ridge, *Origins and Destinations: Family, Class and Education in Modern Britain*, Oxford: Clarendon Press, 1980, p.6

[14] G. Marshall and A. Swift, 'Merit and Mobility: A reply to Peter Saunders', *Sociology*, vol. 30, 1996.

[15] John Rawls, *A Theory of Justice*, Oxford: Oxford University Press, 1972.

[16] Robert Nozick, *Anarchy, State and Utopia*, Oxford: Basil Blackwell, 1974.

[17] F. A. Hayek, *The Constitution of Liberty*, London, Routledge & Kegan Paul, 1960, p. 82.

[18] Geoff Dench, 'Introduction: Reviewing meritocracy' in Geoff Dench (ed.), *The Rise and Rise of Meritocracy*, p. 9.

[19] For a good discussion of this issue, see David Green, *Community Without Politics*, London: Institute of Economic Affairs, 1996, chapter 5.

[20] Nozick, *Anarchy, State and Utopia*, p. 158.

[21] Peter Saunders and Colin Harris, *Privatization and Popular Capitalism*, Buckingham: Open University Press, 1995.

[22] I have subsequently carried out a similar survey in Australia with similar results: the libertarian position was supported by 60 per cent to 26 per cent; the egalitarian position was opposed by 34 per cent to 55 per cent; but the meritocratic position was endorsed by 85 per cent against 7 per cent. See Peter Saunders, 'What is fair about a fair go?', *Policy*, vol. 20, Autumn 2004, pp. 3-10.